Restart English!

—Through Learning Grammar and Culture—

リスタート・イングリッシュ

JN102658

［監修・執筆］安田優／松本恵美／船本弘史／轟里香／デニス・ハーモン

［執筆］長岡亜生／朴育美／奥村玲香／須田久美子／チアノ典子
近藤千代／友田奈津子／吉田明代／杉原由里子

EIHŌSHA

テキストの音声は、弊社 HP　https://www.eihosha.co.jp/
の「テキスト音声ダウンロード」のバナーからダウンロードできます。

はじめに

　このテキストはタイトルが示すように、大学入学を契機として学習者に新たな気持ちで英語学習に取り組んでもらい、グローバル化する社会において必要な知識や英語力を身につけてもらいたいという思いを実現したものです。6年間あるいはそれ以上の英語学習期間を経て、学習者は大学でも英語学習を続けることになります。しかし、これまでに学んだ内容を完璧に習得できないまま大学の授業へ進むことに不安を抱く人もいるのではないでしょうか。特に初級・中級学習者の場合、英語力をステップアップさせるために必要な文法的な基礎知識や語彙・表現力が不足していることも多いかと思います。本テキストはそのような初級・中級レベルの学習者を主な対象にしています。だからと言って、英語学習の初期に扱うような挨拶レベルの内容に焦点を合わせているわけではありません。大学での学習に合わないレベルの例文や容易すぎる内容は学習者の学習意欲を大きく削ぐことになりかねません。このテキストは、学習者がある程度の負荷を感じるとしても、大学生としてのプライドを持って学びを進めることができるだけのレベルを維持したテキストになっています。

　大学における英語学習においては、無尽蔵に時間をかけられるわけではありません。授業内の学習時間、あるいは授業外学習の時間をあわせても、使える時間は限られています。それ故に、効率的に学習を進めることが不可欠です。効果的な授業運営をするうえで大切なことの一つは、学習者が集中して授業に取り組める環境を提供することです。学習者が漫然と授業に参加している状態にならず、限られた時間を最大限に活用できるようにという配慮から、本テキストでは意図的に書き込み式のタスクを多く採り入れています。きっちりとテキストに取り組んだ学習者は、例外なくそれなりの成果を手にすることができます。大学での英語授業を終えた後も、学習者が必要に応じて自分自身でさらなる学びを進められるだけの力を獲得することができているはずです。

　テキストは15ユニットから構成されており、各ユニットには、学習者が足りないところを無理なく補っていけるような、そして各ユニットで扱う文法構造をしっかりと自分のものとして身につけることを可能とする12のタスクが配置されています。例えば、リーディング・タスクへの取り組みが容易になるように、その準備タスクとして、文法構造や語彙・表現に関するインプット作業が用意されています。リーディング素材としては、英米圏の社会や文化に関連する内容を扱ったものを厳選しています。また、英作文のタスクの前には、やはり語彙・表現をインプットするタスクや、文法構造に注目してもらうための Word Order タスクなどが用意されています。そして最後の仕上げとして、学びの内容を発信するタスクが配置されています。多様なインプット作業、アウトプット作業を繰り返すことで、各ユニットにおける学びの内容が定着するはずです。

　本テキストを通じて、多くの学習者が新鮮な気持ちで英語学習に取り組み、現在持っている力を最大限に向上させてくれることを、監修者・執筆者一同願っております。

監修者・執筆者一同

Contents

UNIT 1   The Many Kinds of Roads   1

UNIT 2   Ways to Use the Word "Strong"   7

UNIT 3   How to Count Syllables   13

UNIT 4   Is "Heads Up" Too Informal?   19

UNIT 5   When Was Last Tuesday?   25

UNIT 6   Asking Someone About Their Job   31

UNIT 7   Long Johns and Big Wheels   37

UNIT 8   How Do I Improve My English?   43

UNIT 9   Silent Letters   49

UNIT 10   Anything and Nothing   55

UNIT 11   All About "Develop"   61

UNIT 12   How Do I Continue a Conversation in English?   68

UNIT 13   American Breakfast   74

UNIT 14   Trust or Believe?   80

UNIT 15   How Do You Say Goodbye to a Coworker?   86

解答用紙   92

UNIT 1 ▶▶ The Many Kinds of Roads

00 Grammar：冠詞・名詞・代名詞

●**名詞**　英語では語が指し示す対象の捉え方（種類）によって表し方も変わります：
　☞数える対象…chair/chairs［普通］；effort/efforts［抽象］；family/families［集合］
　☞数えない対象…furniture［総称］；information［抽象］；cheese, water［物質］；Japan［固有］
●**冠詞**　名詞で表す対象が限定されていたり、文脈から特定できたりするかどうかが表現に
　　表れます：
　☞限定される…"*the* ＋ 名詞" の形（the boy/boys, the effort/efforts, the news, the sun）
　☞限定されない…(a) 単数の場合："*a* ＋ 単数形名詞"（a boy, an answer, a piece of news）
　　　　　　　　　(b) 複数の場合："複数形名詞"（boys, answers, efforts, families）
●**代名詞**　置き換えられる名詞の数（単数・複数）に合わせて適切な形を選びましょう：
　☞人称代名詞…<u>Eve</u> waited in <u>her</u> room to greet the <u>guests</u> on <u>their</u> arrival from Paris.
　☞指示代名詞…Listen to <u>this</u>: *Ken's cooking skills* are *those* of a professional.

01 Vocabulary（1）：語彙を増やしましょう。

A. 音声を聴いて、次の表現の発音を確認しましょう。その後、その意味を知らない場合
　は辞書を使って調べましょう。次に全ての語の意味を解答用紙に記入しましょう。

1. city	2. term	3. residential	4. public
5. traffic	6. pave	7. rough	8. connect
9. rural	10. narrow	11. activity	12. plant
13. outdoor	14. relate	15. meter	16. forest
17. center	18. find	19. important	20. general

B. 次の表現は A に入っている単語を定義したものです。それぞれどの単語の定義なのかを考え
　て、このテキストに答えとなる単語を書き込んでみましょう。

定義	答え
1. to discover by searching or by chance	
2. for the use of everyone, not private	
3. small from one side to the other	
4. a large area where trees grow close together	
5. cover a surface with flat stones or bricks	

◎「道」といっても英語には様々な表現があります。ヒロシさんは、その違いについて質問しました。

> **What are the differences between avenues, roads, streets, lanes, drives, ways, trails, boulevards, and highways?**

この質問に対する回答をまずは音声で聴いてみましょう。一回目はテキストの文章に注意を払いながら聴いてみましょう。二回目は音声を聴いて１から８のカッコに入る表現を考えながら聴き、書き入れてみましょう。

Well, that is a good question and one that even some native speakers wonder about.

Let's talk first about roads. (a)A road is a long piece of hard ground built between two places so people can walk, drive or ride easily from one place to the other. Roads can be paved or even made of dirt or stone. Roads (1.   ) in cities, towns and rural areas. They can be large or small. The word "road" is the most general of today's terms and is sometimes used in place of "street" or "highway" or (2.   ) related words.

A street is a public road in a city or town that has buildings on one or both sides of it. Sometimes, we use the word "street" for many kinds of roads. Streets often run (3.   ) avenues, which are wider streets. Let's take the borough of Manhattan in New York City. (b)It has more than two-hundred numbered streets that run east to west. 42nd Street is one example.

Manhattan also has 12 numbered avenues that run north to south. An example is 5th avenue. An avenue is a very wide street, usually inside a city. In Manhattan, most avenues are around 30 meters wide while the streets are (4.   ).

Now, let's talk about smaller streets: lanes and ways. A way is a small side street that is connected to a larger street. And a lane is a very narrow street or (5.   ). Ways and lanes are often found in residential areas.

A boulevard is a wide and usually important city street that often has trees, (6.   ), or flowers planted down its center or along its sides.

"Drive" is used in the name of some public roads. Drives may be big or small. In Manhattan, for example, there is FDR Drive – a six-lane highway. Highways are paved (7.   ) roads that have several lanes for traffic and connect cities, towns and other areas. (c)Vehicles on highways drive at

higher speeds than they do on other kinds of roads.

And finally, we have trails. A trail is usually a rough path（8.　　　　）a field or a forest. Some trails are for people and animals to walk or ride on. Others are for outdoor activities, like hiking and bicycling.

03 本文中の「代名詞」に下線を引いて、それらが何を指しているか考えましょう。

04 Comprehension Questions：

単語の意味をある程度知った上で文章を見ると、理解度が高まることが実感できたのではないでしょうか。では内容の確認をしてみましょう。

次の各文の内容が本文の内容と一致している場合はＴを、一致していない場合はＦを選び、解答用紙に〇をつけましょう。また本文のどの部分を見れば、判断ができるかについても解答用紙に記入しましょう。

（1）Paved roads can be dirty because they are made of stone.
（2）If you walk on a street in a city, you can see buildings on one or both sides of it.
（3）A path or small side street will lead you to a larger street.
（4）A boulevard is wide because it is built in an important city.
（5）Trails are usually for people and animals in a forest, but not for hiking and bicycling.

05 Summary

次の文章は本文の内容をまとめたものです。（　）内に入る表現の最初の文字を書き出してあります。それをヒントに、本文の中から適切な表現を選んで書き入れましょう。

Roads are very important to cities everywhere. They can be（1. p　　　　）or rough. They help people move around and are important for transportation Streets are public roads in a city or town that often have buildings on either side. Roads（2. c　　　　）. the many different places in a city together. There are many names for these roads including: avenues, boulevards, and drives. Additionally, there are trails which are often used for walking or hiking.

06 Translation（1）

本文中の下線部（a）から（c）を日本語に訳してみましょう。訳は解答用紙に書き入れましょう。

07 Translation（2）

次の文中にはこの Unit でこれまでに見てきた表現が含まれています。気をつけながら日本語に訳してみましょう。知らない表現は辞書で調べて、訳は解答用紙に書き入れましょう。

（1） There are a lot of roads that are made of stone in my hometown. *that are made of stone：roads を説明。
（2） Our teacher told us to decorate the picture frame with some flowers on one side or both of it. *tell ＋人＋ to- 動詞の原形：「人に〜するようにと言う」という意味。
（3） Phone calls are connected to the nurse center, not directly to the doctor. *be 動詞＋過去分詞：受動態で「〜されている」という意味。
（4） Some earlier species of animals are found in the small island.
（5） At this university, some courses are for all students, while others are for those from overseas.

■ 休　憩

● a や the といった冠詞がつくかつかないかは、その名詞をどんな意味で使うかによって変わります。例えば school を具体的な「場・施設」の意味で言うと a school（例：a school built in 2000「2000 年に建てられた学校」）のように冠詞がつきますが、学校での活動シーンやそこで過ごす時間として捉えれば冠詞はつきません。
☞ I go to school.「通学する（＝ 学びに行く）」
☞ She is still at school.「在学中です」

08 Word Order：

A. 次の [　] 内の表現を日本語に合うように並べ替えてみましょう。名詞の用法に注意し，代名詞も必要に応じて使ってください。冒頭は大文字で書き始め、答えは解答用紙に記入しましょう。

（1） その大統領は環境問題に関するたくさんの意見に耳を貸さなかった。
[many opinions about,　environmental issues,　the President,　lend an ear to,　didn't].
（2） ビッグバン理論を支持するたくさんの証拠がある。
[there is,　to support,　a lot of,　the big bang theory,　evidence].
（3） 救助隊は被災者にパンを 2 切れずつ与えた。
[two pieces of bread,　each of the victims,　the rescue team,　to,　gave].

（4）君に必要なのは自分自身の弱さを克服する意志だけだ。
[all you need,　weaknesses,　overcome,　your own,　is the will to].

（5）通りのどちら側にも街路樹はなかった。
[either side of,　I could not find,　the road,　any boulevard trees on].

B. 並べ替えたものが合っているどうかを、音声を聴いて確かめてみましょう。間違いがある場合は、自分の答えがなぜ間違いなのかを考えてみましょう。

09 **Vocabulary（2）：語彙を増やしましょう。**

次の日本語表現の意味に合う英語表現を結びつけてみましょう。選んだ答えの表現を解答欄に書き入れましょう。

1.　ドイツ	2.　いつの日か	3.　制度
4.　人類	5.　教育	6.　火星
7.　〜の仲間に入る	8.　〜ごと	9.　必ず〜する

 語 群 education,　join,　Mars,　system,　make sure to,　humankind,　someday,　every, Germany

> Vocabulary（2）の表現を使って、次の日本語を英語にしてみよう。ヒントを参考にしてみましょう。

10 Composition：作った英文は解答用紙に記入しましょう。

(1) 私は必ず1週間おきに医者に診てもらいます。＊「2週間ごとに」と読み替えましょう。

(2) そのダンスチームには誰でも仲間に入れます。＊anyone を主語にして書いてみましょう。

(3) 日本の教育制度とドイツの教育制度は違う。＊代名詞を適切に使いましょう。

(4) いつの日か人類は火星に到達するだろう。＊a, an, the が必要かどうかに注意。

11 Exercise：次の2つの設問について考えてみましょう。

(1) 英語は、同じ形の語が、名詞としても動詞としても使われる場合があります。ある語が名詞として使われているのかどうかを判断する手掛かりの一つとして、冠詞があります。次の文がそれぞれどのような意味かを、下線部の語が名詞かどうかに注意して、考えてみましょう。

・I walk to work every day.

・Let's go for a walk.

・The following is a digest of Japan newspapers published on March 11, 2021.

・He read and digested the difficult book.

・He says that the world has a responsibility to end the war in that country.

・I have to finish this report by the end of this month.

(2) 次の名詞の前に、a か an のどちらが入るかを考えてみましょう。

( ) book   ( ) cat   ( ) orange

( ) girl   ( ) house   ( ) story

( ) air conditioner ( ) eagle   ( ) actor

12 Speed Writing／Discussion／Presentation

(1) クラス内で指示された課題について、クラスメートと話し合ってみましょう。

(2) 話し合いの内容をもとにして、指定された時間内に指定された語数以上で自分の考えを書いてみましょう。この Unit で学んだ文法事項を意識して文章を作ってください。それ以外は文法事項にこだわり過ぎず、できる限り多くの英文を気楽に書いてみましょう。

(3) 自分の考えた文章をクラスメートの前で発表してみましょう。

00 **Grammar**：形容詞・副詞・前置詞について

●形容詞は名詞を修飾し、その使い方にはいくつかのパターンがあります。

（a）は最も基本的なパターンで、下線部分が形容詞です。

☞（a）Racial discrimination is very widespread in the United States.

人種差別はアメリカでまん延している。

racial は名詞の前に置かれ、discrimination を修飾しています（限定用法）。widespread は動詞の後に置かれ、差別がどのような状態にあるかを説明しています（叙述用法）。

●副詞には形容詞や文全体を修飾する役割などの機能があります。（a）では very が widespread を、（b）では extremely が difficult を修飾しています。

☞（b）Age discrimination is extremely difficult to define.

年齢差別は定義するのがとても難しい。

●前置詞は（代）名詞の前に置かれ、その（代）名詞の意味を補います。よく使われるものは of、for、by、to、from、with、in などです。例文（a）の in は場所を表す前置詞。例文（c）の in は範囲を限定しています。また sometimes は頻度を表す副詞です。

☞（c）Ethnic minorities sometimes face discrimination in employment.

少数民族の人々は時々、雇用において差別に直面する。

01 **Vocabulary**（1）：語彙を増やしましょう。

A. 音声を聴いて、次の表現の発音を確認しましょう。その後、その意味を知らない場合は辞書を使って調べましょう。次に全ての語の意味を解答用紙に記入しましょう。 **05**

1. describe	2. power	3. person	4. necessarily
5. teeth/tooth	6. quality	7. bone	8. muscle
9. wind	10. event	11. issue	12. happen
13. future	14. even	15. win	16. imagine
17. paint	18. smell	19. understand	20. against

B. 次の表現は A に入っている単語を定義したものです。それぞれどの単語の定義なのかを考えて、このテキストに答えとなる単語を書き込んでみましょう。

定義	答え
1. ability to control people and events	
2. to know why or how something happens or works	
3. a man, woman, or child	

定義	答え
4. to achieve first position and/or get a prize in a competition, etc. *achieve：達成する、*prize：賞、*competition：競争	
5. how good or bad something is	

02 Reading／Listening：文章の大まかな意味をつかんでみましょう。

◎ "strong" という形容詞について、マサルさんは次のような質問をしました。

> Hello!
> We use the word "strong" to describe a person and a team.
> Can we use it to describe a country?

この質問に対する回答をまずは音声で聴いてみましょう。一回目はテキストの文章に注意を払いながら聴いてみましょう。二回目は音声を聴いて1から8のカッコに入る表現を考えながら聴き、書き入れてみましょう。

As you know, "strong" is an adjective. It describes something that has (1.　　　　) or something that cannot easily be broken, damaged or destroyed.

You are right. English speakers use the word "strong" to describe a person or a team. We can also use it to describe a country. However, (a)describing something with the adjective "strong" does not necessarily mean it is good. Strong can (2.　　　　) things that are good or bad.

"Strong" as a good quality

In fact, almost anything can be strong. For example, people can be strong. But things like teeth, bones and muscles can be (3.　　　　) too. The wind can be strong. Here is an example: The weather report says there will be strong (4.　　　　) tomorrow.

(b)"Strong" can describe feelings also. You can have a strong feeling about someone, some event or issue. You may even feel you know what may happen in the future, like this:

I have a strong feeling about our (5.　　　　) winning the championship.

"Strong" for bad qualities

"Strong" can also be used to describe bad qualities. For example, imagine you painted a room and your (6.　　　　) comes in and says:

oh!

The paint (7.　　　　) is too strong. Open the

window, please!

"Strong" can mean something that is hard to fight against. Many students might understand this example:

When I sit in the（8.　　　　）for a long time, I have a strong desire to sleep.
(c) So, the adjective "strong" can be used to describe good things and bad ones, too.

03　本文中に出てくる「形容詞」を探して、下線を引いてみましょう。

04　Comprehension Questions：

単語の意味をある程度知った上で文章を見ると、理解度が高まることが実感できたのではないでしょうか。では内容の確認をしてみましょう。

次の各文の内容が本文の内容と一致している場合はＴを、一致していない場合はＦを選び、解答用紙に〇をつけましょう。また本文のどの部分を見れば、判断ができるかについても解答用紙に記入しましょう。

（1） English speakers cannot use the adjective "strong" to describe a country.
（2） The word "strong" does not always mean it is good.
（3） "Strong" can mean something that is difficult to fight against.
（4） You can say, "the paint smell is too strong."
（5） The adjective "strong" can be used to describe your desire to sleep.

05　Summary
次の文章は本文の内容をまとめたものです。（　　）内に入る表現の最初の文字を書き出してあります。それをヒントに、本文の中から適切な表現を選んで書き入れましょう。

The English word "strong" can be used to（1.　d　　　　　）many things. You can use it as an adjective for things such as（2.　t　　　　）, bones, and muscles. Strong does not only have a good meaning. It can also be used to explain bad things like the smell of paint.

06　Translation（1）
本文中の下線部（a）から（c）を日本語に訳してみましょう。訳は解答用紙に書き入れましょう。

次の文中にはこの Unit でこれまでに見てきた表現が含まれています。気をつけながら日本語に訳してみましょう。知らない表現は辞書で調べて、訳は解答用紙に書き入れましょう。

（1）Strong winds are forecasted in the southern area for the next few days.
*be 動詞 ＋ 過去分詞：受動態で「〜されている」という意味。*forecast の過去分詞は forecast と forecasted どちらもあり得ます。

（2）Did you have a good time at the party?

（3）My father only buys high-quality wine.

（4）As you know, money doesn't necessarily buy happiness.

（5）I imagine that she is under a lot of pressure right now.

■ 休憩 ------------------------------------

● The classroom is full of teenagers.（その教室はティーンエイジャーでいっぱいです）という文では "full" という形容詞は叙述用法で使われていますが、次のように名詞の後に置かれる場合もあります。
☞ The classroom full of teenagers became suddenly silent.
ティーンエイジャーでいっぱいの教室が突然静かになった。

08 Word Order：

A. 次の ［ ］ 内の表現を日本語に合うように並べ替えてみましょう。形容詞、副詞、前置詞を意識しながら考えてみてください。冒頭は大文字で書き始め、答えは解答用紙に記入しましょう。

（1）その先生は社会的不公正を正す多くの方法の一つとして、アファーマティブ・アクションを説明した。*social：社会的な、*injustice：不公正

[social injustice, one of many ways to correct, the teacher described, affirmative action as].

（2）児童虐待は、たいてい見えないところに隠されている。*abuse：虐待

[from view, child, is usually, abuse, hidden].

（3）今日、僕のオフィスでおかしなことがあった。

[happened in, office today, my, a funny thing].

（4） 100 人以上がその新しい提案に反対する票を投じた。 *vote：投票する、*proposal：提案
［ the new proposal,　100 people,　voted against,　more than ］.
（5） その研究チームは、ものすごい速さでワクチンを開発した。 　　*vaccines：ワクチン、*develop：開発する
［ warp speed,　developed,　the research team,　vaccines at ］.

B. 並べ替えたものが合っているどうかを、音声を聴いて確かめてみましょう。間違いがある場合は、自分の答えがなぜ間違いなのかを考えてみましょう。

09　Vocabulary（2）：語彙を増やしましょう。

次の日本語表現の意味に合う英語表現を結びつけてみましょう。選んだ答えの表現を解答欄に書き入れましょう。

1．おじいさん	2．〜すぎる	3．子供時代
4．役に立つ	5．教室	6．宗教
7．意見	8．〜に影響を与える	9．〜にとって

語 群　childhood,　religion,　opinions,　too,　useful,　for,　have an influence on,　grandfather,　classroom

> Vocabulary（2）の表現を使って、次の日本語を英語にしてみよう。ヒントを参考にしてみましょう。

10 Composition：作った英文は解答用紙に記入しましょう。

（1）私のおじいさんは、僕の子供時代に強い影響を与えた。 *have の過去形の had を使ってみましょう。

（2）教室でスマートフォンを使うことは、時々、役に立つ。 *Using smartphones で始めてましょう。
*in the classroom という表現を使ってみましょう。 *副詞は be 動詞の後に置きましょう。

（3）私のお父さんは、宗教についてしっかりした考えを持っている。
*strong と about を使ってみましょう。

（4）このコーヒーは僕には濃すぎる。 *〜過ぎる＝too：形容詞 strong の前に置いてみましょう。

11 Exercise：日本語に合うように、次の文の（ ）に入れるのに最適な表現を選びましょう。

（1）It is（ ）annoying when a train is late and there is no explanation.
電車が遅れて、説明がない時には、本当にイライラする。

（a）rarely　　　　（b）really

（2）The COVID-19 pandemic completely changed our lives（ ）just one week.
コロナウィルスの流行は、たった一週間で私たちの生活を完全に変えた。

（a）in　　　　（b）on

（3）She（ ）claims that she is a victim of age discrimination.
彼女はいつも（＝100％）自分が年齢差別の犠牲者だと主張する。

（a）always　　　　（b）often

12 Speed Writing／Discussion／Presentation

（1）クラス内で指示された課題について、クラスメートと話し合ってみましょう。

（2）話し合いの内容をもとにして、指定された時間内に指定された語数以上で自分の考えを書いてみましょう。この Unit で学んだ文法事項を意識して文章を作ってください。それ以外は文法事項にこだわり過ぎず、できる限り多くの英文を気楽に書いてみましょう。

（3）自分の考えた文章をクラスメートの前で発表してみましょう。

00 **Grammar**：第一文型、第二文型、第三文型について

●英文を構成する主な要素は S（主語）、V（動詞）、O（目的語）、C（補語）の４つです。
英文はこの構成要素の組み合わせにより、5 つの文型に分けることができます。まずはこ
の 5 文型の基本的な最初の 3 つから始めましょう。

☞第一文型〈S + V〉は「S は〔が〕V する」という意味の最もシンプルな文型です。

(1) <u>Babies</u> <u>cry</u>.　赤ん坊は泣くものだ。
　　　　 S　　 V

☞第二文型〈S + V + C〉は第一文型と異なり動詞の後に補語がきて初めて成立します。

(2) <u>That chair</u> <u>looks</u> <u>comfortable</u>.　その椅子は心地よさそうに見える。
　　　　　 S　　 　V　　 　C

ポイントは、補語が主語を説明していて、S = C の関係が成立することです。

☞第三文型〈S + V + O〉は「主語 + 動詞 + 目的語」で成立します。

(3) <u>My mother</u> <u>bought</u> <u>a new car</u>. 私の母は新しい車を買いました。
　　　　 S　　 　 V　　 　 O

日本語の「…を」に当たる部分が目的語です。また、この文型は第二文型〈S + V + C〉
と異なり、S = O の関係は成立しません。

01 **Vocabulary（1）：語彙を増やしましょう。**

A. 音声を聴いて、次の表現の発音を確認しましょう。その後、その意味を知らない場合
は辞書を使って調べましょう。次に全ての語の意味を解答用紙に記入しましょう。

1. syllable	2. pronunciation	3. divide	4. decide
5. vowel	6. sound	7. machine	8. letter
9. spelling	10. method	11. counting	12. chin
13. rest	14. drop	15. clap	16. autumn
17. fun	18. close	19. following	20. carefully

B. 次の表現は A に入っている単語を定義したものです。それぞれどの単語の定義なのかを考え
て、このテキストに答えとなる単語を書き込んでみましょう。

定義	答え
1. any one of the parts into which a word is naturally divided when it is pronounced	
2. the act of forming words from letters	
3. a letter（such as a, e, i, o, u, and sometimes y in English）that makes a specific sound	

定義	答え
4.　the part of the face below the mouth and above the neck	
5.　to hit the palms of your hands together usually more than once 　　*palms：手のひら	

02　Reading／Listening：文章の大まかな意味をつかんでみましょう。

◎音節について、ナツコさんは次のような質問をしました。

Hello!
Today our question is related to pronunciation. How can we recognize the syllables in a word? Would you mind explaining the rules?

この質問に対する回答をまずは音声で聴いてみましょう。一回目はテキストの文章に注意を払いながら聴いてみましょう。二回目は音声を聴いて 1 から 8 のカッコに入る表現を考えながら聴き、書き入れてみましょう。

Understanding syllables helps *a lot* with（1.　　　　　）. As we speak, if we miss or add a syllable to a word, people may not be able to understand us.

When we say a word, the sounds we create naturally divide the word into parts. We call these parts "syllables." For example, the word "machine" has two parts: ma-chine.（a）The word "important" has three parts: im-por-tant.

The number of（2.　　　　　）in a word is decided by its number of **vowel** sounds. For example, in the word "machine," there are two vowel sounds: [ə] and [i].

It is important to know that one syllable can have more than one（3.　　　　　）letter. For example, the word "room" has two vowel letters: *o* and *o*. But together, they make only one vowel sound: [u:]. This explains why "room" has only（4.　　　　　）syllable.（b）We decide syllables by sound, not spelling.

Ok, here are two easy methods for（5.　　　　　）syllables.

One that I like is the **chin** method. Here is how to do it: Rest your hand under your（6.　　　　　）and say a word slowly. How many times does your chin（7.　　　　　）onto your hand? That is the number of syllables.

chin method

Another is the **clap** method. To use it, say the word

and (8.　　　　　) your hands together each time you hear a vowel sound. For example, take the word "autumn": au-tumn. (c)That's two vowel sounds, so it's two syllables even though autumn has three vowel letters: *a*, *u* and *u*.

03 本文中に出てくる「第三文型」を三つ探して、下線を引いてみましょう。

04 Comprehension Questions：

> 単語の意味をある程度知った上で文章を見ると、理解度が高まることが実感できたのではないでしょうか。では内容の確認をしてみましょう。

次の各文の内容が本文の内容と一致している場合は T を、一致していない場合は F を選び、解答用紙に〇をつけましょう。また本文のどの部分を見れば、判断ができるかについても解答用紙に記入しましょう。

（1） Syllables are the number of vowel sounds in a word.
（2） The word "machine" has three syllables.
（3） Syllables are decided not only by sound but also by spelling.
（4） The chin method gives you the number of syllables when you pronounce a word slowly.
（5） The clap method is much easier to count syllables than the chin method.

05 Summary
次の文章は本文の内容をまとめたものです。（　）内に入る表現の最初の文字を書き出してあります。それをヒントに、本文の中から適切な表現を選んで書き入れましょう。

> （1. S　　　　　　　） help with pronunciation. They are the naturally divided parts of a word. Syllables are decided by the number of （2. v　　　　　　） in a word. Two good ways to count syllables is the chin and clap method.

06 Translation（1）
本文中の下線部（a）から（c）を日本語に訳してみましょう。訳は解答用紙に書き入れましょう。

07 **Translation(2)**

次の文中にはこの Unit でこれまでに見てきた表現が含まれています。気をつけながら日本語に訳してみましょう。知らない表現は辞書で調べて、訳は解答用紙に書き入れましょう。

(1) Is my pronunciation correct?
(2) She will decide as she pleases.
(3) "Theatre" is a British spelling.
(4) Tears dropped from my grandfather's eyes.
(5) Close the windows.

■ 休憩 ·······

●第二文型で使用される動詞は、「状態」、「感覚」を表す語が用いられます。
例えば、be 動詞、become, remain, appear, get, feel, look, seem などが使われます。
☞状態型：The restaurant remains closed. その店は閉まっている。
☞感覚型：This towel feels soft. このタオルは柔らかい。

08 **Word Order：**

A. 次の [ ] 内の表現を日本語に合うように並べ替えてみましょう。第一文型〈S ＋ V〉、第二文型〈S ＋ V ＋ C〉、第三文型〈S ＋ V ＋ O〉の語順に注意しながら考えてください。冒頭は大文字で書き始め、答えは解答用紙に記入しましょう。

(1) その子熊はもっと大きくなるだろう。 *第二文型
[will, the bear cub, much, get, bigger].
(2) 鳥は歌い花は咲く。 *第一文型
[the birds, bloom, sing, the flowers, and].
(3) 私は興味深い歴史の本を見つけた。 *第三文型
[I, an interesting, found, history book].
(4) 赤いドレスは彼女によく似合っている。 *第二文型
[she, in her, looks wonderful, red dress].

（5）甘い香りがキッチンをいっぱいにした。*第三文型

[saturated,　sweet,　the kitchen,　odors].

B. 並べ替えたものが合っているどうかを、音声を聴いて確かめてみましょう。間違いがある場合
は、自分の答えがなぜ間違いなのかを考えてみましょう。

09 Vocabulary（2）：語彙を増やしましょう。

次の日本語表現の意味に合う英語表現を結びつけてみましょう。選んだ答えの表現を解答欄に書き
入れましょう。

1. 鐘（の音）	2. 澄んだ	3. （パンやケーキなどを）焼く
4. おばさん	5. 〜の計画を立てる	6. 終える
7. 明日	8. 輝く	9. 〜のように

語 群　bell,　shine,　aunt,　make plans for,　clear,　like,　bake,　finish,　tomorrow

Vocabulary（2）の表現を使って、次の日本語を英語
にしてみよう。ヒントを参考にしてみましょう。

10 Composition：作った英文は解答用紙に記入しましょう。

(1) 鐘の音が澄んで聞こえる。 *鐘を主語にしましょう。
(2) おばさんはたくさんのフルーツケーキを焼いた。 *a lot of を使いましょう。
(3) 私たちは夕食を食べ終え、明日の計画を立てた。
(4) 月がランプのように輝いている。 *lamp

11 Exercise：the chin method/ the clap method を使って次の 5 つの単語の音節をカウントし、解答欄にその数を書き込みましょう。

1. tomorrow	2. recorded	3. struts	4. heard	5. nothing

12 Speed Writing／Discussion／Presentation

(1) クラス内で指示された課題について、クラスメートと話し合ってみましょう。

(2) 話し合いの内容をもとにして、指定された時間内に指定された語数以上で自分の考えを書いてみましょう。この Unit で学んだ文法事項を意識して文章を作ってください。それ以外は文法事項にこだわり過ぎず、できる限り多くの英文を気楽に書いてみましょう。

(3) 自分の考えた文章をクラスメートの前で発表してみましょう。

UNIT 4 ▶▶ Is "Heads Up" Too Informal?

00 Grammar：第四文型・第五文型について

● 第一・第二・第三文型（Unit 3）に引き続き、第四・第五文型を学習しましょう。

☞ 第四文型：〈S＋V＋O₁＋O₂〉　主語＋動詞のあと目的語を 2 つ伴う文型で、「S は O₁ に O₂ を V する」「S は O₁ のために O₂ を V する」などの意味をあらわします。

（1）<u>Anne</u> <u>gave</u> <u>her mother</u> <u>a present</u>.　アンはお母さんにプレゼントをあげた。
　　　 S　　V　　O₁（～に）　O₂（～を）

☞ 第五文型：〈S＋V＋O＋C〉　主語＋動詞のあとに目的語＋補語がくる文型で、「S は O が C だと V する」や「S は O を C（の状態）に V する」などの意味をあらわします。

（2）<u>The message</u> <u>made</u> <u>me</u> <u>happy</u>.　そのメッセージは私を幸せにした。
　　　 S　　　　　 V　　 O　　C　　（メッセージのおかげで私は幸せになった。）

01 Vocabulary（1）：語彙を増やしましょう。

A. 音声を聴いて、次の表現の発音を確認しましょう。その後、その意味を知らない場合は辞書を使って調べましょう。次に全ての語の意味を解答用紙に記入しましょう。

1. term	2. informal	3. common	4. almost
5. situation	6. noun	7. send	8. company
9. president	10. report	11. process	12. worth
13. note	14. coworker	15. warn	16. express
17. imagine	18. move	19. supervisor	20. aware

B. 次の表現は A に入っている単語を定義したものです。それぞれどの単語の定義なのかを考えて、このテキストに答えとなる単語を書き込んでみましょう。

定義	答え
1. relaxed in tone or not suited for serious or official speech and writing　*suited for：～に適した、*tone：調子	
2. noticing that something is present, or that something is happening *notice：～に気づく、*present：存在している	
3. to tell someone that something bad or dangerous may happen, so that they can avoid it or prevent it　*avoid：～を避ける、*prevent：～を防ぐ	
4. someone who works with you and has a similar position	
5. happening often and to many people or in many places	

◎ "heads up" という表現について、アキさんは次のような質問をしました。

> Could you tell me what else I can use instead of "heads up?" That term is considered informal; therefore, I would like to know the formal word for "heads up."

この質問に対する回答をまずは音声で聴いてみましょう。一回目はテキストの文章に注意を払いながら聴いてみましょう。二回目は音声を聴いて 1 から 8 のカッコに入る表現を考えながら聴き、書き入れてみましょう。

12

Let us look closely at this expression and other ways to say it.

Meaning of "heads up"

As you said, the term "heads up" is (1.　　　　). However, it is so common in American English that we use it in almost every (2.　　　　).

"Heads up" can be used as a (3.　　　　). It sends a message that says something is going to happen. Here is an example:

She gave him a heads up that the company's president would be visiting the office.

Also, you can ask for a "heads up" by asking someone to report when they are in the (4.　　　　) of doing something.

Can you give me a heads up about how much time you will need for that project?

Other ways to say "heads up"

It is worth (5.　　　　) that "heads up" is a common expression Americans use with friends, family, coworkers and even in business meetings. (a)But there are other ways to express the idea. One word you can use in place of "heads up" is "warn":

She warned him that the company's president would be visiting the office.

Another way to express the idea is with the word "let" when you want to give or get information:

(b)*Please let me know how much time you will need for that project.*

(6.　　　　) that your company is (7.　　　　) to a new office and your (8.　　　　) is sending you an email. The message could "make you aware" of something or "draw your attention" to something, as we hear in these examples:

(c)*I want to make you aware that we are moving our office.*

> *I wanted to draw your attention to the move of our office.*

03 本文中に出てくる「第四、五文型をとる動詞（**give, make**）」を探して、下線を引いて みましょう。

04 **Comprehension Questions**：

> 単語の意味をある程度知った上で文章を見ると、理解度が高まることが実感でき たのではないでしょうか。では内容の確認をしてみましょう。

次の各文の内容が本文の内容と一致している場合はTを、一致していない場合はF を選び、解答用紙に〇をつけましょう。また本文のどの部分を見れば、判断ができ るかについても解答用紙に記入しましょう。

（1）You use "heads up" in very formal situations in the US.
（2）The phrase "heads up" expresses the idea that something is not going to happen.
（3）There are several other ways of saying "heads up."
（4）It is not a good idea to use "heads up" in a business meeting.
（5）When you give someone a heads up about something, you let them know about it.

05 **Summary**

次の文章は本文の内容をまとめたものです。（ ）内に入る表現の最初の文字を書き出してありま す。それをヒントに、本文の中から適切な表現を選んで書き入れましょう。

> The informal term "heads up" is commonly used in everyday American English to often
> （1. w   ）others something is happening. There are other ways to（2. e   ）this
> such as "make you aware" or "draw your attention" to something. These other ways are
> often used in company messages.

06 **Translation（1）**

本文中の下線部（a）から（c）を日本語に訳してみましょう。訳は解答用紙に書き入れましょう。

07 Translation（2）

次の文中にはこの Unit でこれまでに見てきた表現が含まれています。気をつけながら日本語に訳してみましょう。知らない表現は辞書で調べて、訳は解答用紙に書き入れましょう。

（1）We had an informal discussion after the lecture.

（2）It is a common mistake among English learners.

（3）Most people are aware of the problem.

（4）Don't worry. I won't let you down.

（5）Payment must be made within ten days.　*must：「〜しなければならない」という意味の助動詞 (Unit 8)

■ 休憩 --

●第四文型と第五文型　見分け方のヒント
第五文型〈S＋V＋O＋C〉では〈目的語 O ＝ 補語 C〉の関係が成立します。冒頭の例文（2）The message made me happy. では、me ＝ happy（私 ＝ 幸せ）。他方、2つの目的語が並ぶ第四文型では、O₁と O₂ の間にこのような関係は成立しません。例文（1）Anne gave her mother a present. では、her mother ≠ a present となりますね。

08 Word Order：

A. 次の〔　〕内の表現を日本語に合うように並べ替えてみましょう。目的語の位置に注意しながら考えてみてください。冒頭は大文字で書き始め、答えは解答用紙に記入しましょう。

13

（1）この本は読む価値があるとあなたは思いますか。

［this book,　do you,　is,　think,　worth reading］?

（2）マーガリンは、バターの代わりに使うことができます。

［be used,　of butter,　can,　margarine,　in place］.

（3）なにかお飲み物をさしあげましょうか。

［to drink,　can I,　get,　something,　you］?

（4）医者のせいで患者はとても緊張していた。

［the doctor,　his patient,　made,　nervous,　very］.

（5）ファイルを添付したメールをお送りします。

[an email, send you, we, with a file attached, will].

B. 並べ替えたものが合っているどうかを、音声を聴いて確かめてみましょう。間違いがある場合
は、自分の答えがなぜ間違いなのかを考えてみましょう。

09 Vocabulary（2）：語彙を増やしましょう。

次の日本語表現の意味に合う英語表現を結びつけてみましょう。選んだ答えの表現を解答欄に書き
入れましょう。

1．もってくる	2．新聞	3．〜を…の状態にしておく
4．電灯、電気	5．どうか、どうぞ	6．受け取る
7．荷物、小包	8．〜を…だと思う、感じる	9．快適な、居心地のよい

語群　find, comfortable, bring, leave, light, newspaper, package, please, receive

Vocabulary（2）の表現を使って、次の日本語を英語
にしてみよう。ヒントを参考にしてみましょう。

10 Composition：作った英文は解答用紙に記入しましょう。

（1）私に新聞をもってきてくれませんか。*疑問文で丁寧に依頼する表現を使いましょう。
（2）あなたのために、電気をつけておきますね。*「これから〜する」という未来の形で表現します。
（3）荷物を受け取ったら、私に知らせてください。*丁寧な命令文。「〜したら」は「〜するとき」と考えましょう。
（4）私は、その部屋はとても居心地がよいと思った。*動詞は過去形を用います。

11 Exercise（Body Parts Idioms）：今回学んだ "heads up" のように、英語には身体の部位を使った表現がいろいろあります。下線部の意味に合うものを下から選び、ヒントも参考に文全体の意味を考えてみましょう。

（1）You're pulling my leg! I know you didn't win the lottery.　*win a lottery：宝くじに当たる
（2）The politician puts his foot in his mouth whenever he opens his mouth.　*politician：政治家
（3）He was going to ask her out, but he got cold feet and said nothing.　*ask～out：～をデートに誘う
（4）I told her to keep her chin up and work hard for the team.　*work hard：一生懸命取り組む・励む
（5）We are keeping our fingers crossed that she is going to pass the exam. *pass the exam：試験に合格する

［ へまをする、～をからかう、幸運を祈る、おじけづく、元気を出す ］

12 Speed Writing／Discussion／Presentation

（1）クラス内で指示された課題について、クラスメートと話し合ってみましょう。

（2）話し合いの内容をもとにして、指定された時間内に指定された語数以上で自分の考えを書いてみましょう。この Unit で学んだ文法事項を意識して文章を作ってください。それ以外は文法事項にこだわり過ぎず、できる限り多くの英文を気楽に書いてみましょう。

（3）自分の考えた文章をクラスメートの前で発表してみましょう。

00 **Grammar：Be 動詞について**

●Be 動詞とは、主語の「属性・状態」を示したり、「A は B である」のようにふたつのもの
を同定したり、「(〜に) ある・いる」のように主語の「存在」を示したりするときに使う
動詞です。別の動詞を進行形や受身形で用いるときにも使います。
☞まずは、Be 動詞の活用を確認してみましょう。

	現在形	過去形	過去分詞形
一人称：I	am	was	(have) been
二人称：you	are	were	(have) been
三人称単数：he, she, it	is	was	(has) been
三人称複数：they	are	were	(have) been

01 **Vocabulary（1）：語彙を増やしましょう。**

A. 音声を聴いて、次の表現の発音を確認しましょう。その後、その意味を知らない場合
は辞書を 使って調べましょう。次に全ての語句の意味を解答用紙に記入しましょう。

(14)

1. native	2. misunderstand	3. expression	4. adjective
5. day of the week	6. depending on	7. means	8. recent
9. imagine	10. probably	11. further	12. make certain of
13. exact	14. somewhat	15. unusual	16. suppose
17. clear	18. regularly	19. date	20. current

B. 次の表現は A に入っている単語を定義したものです。それぞれどの単語の定義なのかを考え
て、このテキストに答えとなる単語を書き込んでみましょう。

定義	答え
1. to understand something or somebody wrongly	
2. that happened only a short time ago	
3. not ordinary or normal *ordinary：普通の	
4. sure or definite; without any doubts or confusion *definite：確実な、*doubt：不確かさ、*confusion：あいまいさ	
5. a particular day of the month or year *particular：特定の	

◎ "last Tuesday" や "next Tuesday" という表現について、アキヨさんは次の質問をしました。

Do you use the phrase "last Tuesday?" If so, what does it mean? Does it mean "on Tuesday last week" or "on Tuesday this week?" I have the same question for "next Tuesday."

この質問に対する回答をまずは音声で聴いてみましょう。一回目はテキストの文章に注意を払いながら聴いてみましょう。二回目は音声を聴いて 1 から 8 のカッコに入る表現を考えながら聴き、書き入れてみましょう。

15

That is a great question. Even native English speakers can (1.   ) these expressions. "Last" and "next" are both adjectives. When we use them with a day of the week, their meaning can change (2.   ) the time we are speaking.

Last

"Last" (3.   ) the most recent. If today is Wednesday, and I tell you, "I talked with her last Tuesday," you might think I meant I talked with her eight days ago. (a) The reason is if I had talked with her only one day ago, I would have said, "I talked with her yesterday." So, when I say, "I talked with her last Tuesday," I mean the Tuesday of the week before.

Now (4.   ) that today is Thursday or Friday. That means Tuesday is only a few days ago. Here is what I would probably say: "I talked to her on Tuesday."

But now imagine it is Saturday or Sunday, a little (5.   ) away from the day I talked with her. If I say, "I talked with her last Tuesday" you would probably ask me, "Do you mean on Tuesday of this week?" to make (6.   ) of the exact day.

Note that people in different places where English is spoken use these expressions in somewhat different ways. (b) So it is not unusual for native speakers to ask questions when they hear someone using "last" or "next" with a day.

Next

"Next" means "coming after the one that just came or happened." (7.   ) you get a message by email that says, "The meeting is next Tuesday." Since today is Wednesday, it is clear that the meeting will be in six days. (c) But if you have not been reading your email regularly and you get

the message on Monday, you may want to check the date on the message. If you did not look at the (8.   ) of the email, you would probably think the meeting is in eight days. The reason is that the writer would have said, "The meeting is tomorrow" if it was on Tuesday of the current week.

03 本文中に出てくる「Be 動詞」を探して、下線を引いてみましょう。

04 Comprehension Questions：

> 単語の意味をある程度知った上で文章を見ると、理解度が高まることが実感できたのではないでしょうか。では内容の確認をしてみましょう。

次の各文の内容が本文の内容と一致している場合は T を、一致していない場合は F を選び、解答用紙に○をつけましょう。また本文のどの部分を見れば、判断ができるかについても解答用紙に記入しましょう。

(1) Native English speakers always understand the expression "last Tuesday" correctly.
(2) When an English speaker talks about what happened a day before, they would use the expression "yesterday" instead of "last Tuesday."
(3) When someone talks about what happened four or five days ago, and uses the expression "last Tuesday," the listener can be unsure of the exact day the speaker means.
(4) People in the United States and people in New Zealand may use the same English expression in somewhat different ways.
(5) Unlike the expression "last Tuesday," people can always be certain of when exactly "next Tuesday" means.

05 Summary
次の文章は本文の内容をまとめたものです。（　）内に入る表現の最初の文字を書き出してあります。それをヒントに、本文の中から適切な表現を選んで書き入れましょう。

> The (1. e   ) "last Tuesday" and "next Tuesday" can be difficult to understand. Even native speakers can misunderstand the (2. e   ) meaning depending on when it is used. In general, "last" means the most recent time, and "next" means coming after, but these expressions are not exact.

06 Translation（1）

本文中の下線部（a）から（c）を日本語に訳してみましょう。訳は解答用紙に書き入れましょう。

*（a）If I had..., I would have... 仮定法で「もしも…したのだとしたら、…していただろう」という意味になる。
*（b）to ask questions「質問すること」という意味になる。このような動詞の使い方を不定詞と呼ぶ。
 hear someone using...「誰かが…を使っているのを聞く」。

07 Translation（2）

次の文中にはこの Unit でこれまでに見てきた表現が含まれています。気をつけながら日本語に訳してみましょう。知らない表現は辞書で調べて、訳は解答用紙に書き入れましょう。

（1）How successful you will be in the future depends on how hard you work now. *How から in the future までが主部。*depend on：「～次第」という意味。
（2）I will call you next week, probably on Tuesday.
（3）I am somewhat confused about the changes that are taking place. *take place：「起こる」という意味。
（4）I am sorry, but I am not quite clear on what you mean.
（5）Communication devices in the 1990s were very different from the current ones.

■ 休憩

●英語の Be 動詞とぴったり意味や用法が一致するような日本語はありませんが、英語では非常に重要な動詞です。Be 動詞が含まれる、次の有名なフレーズの意味を考えてみましょう。
☞ Time is money.（フランクリンの格言）
☞ I think, therefore I am.（フランスの哲学者デカルトの言葉）

08 Word Order：

A. 次の［ ］内の表現を日本語に合うように並べ替えてみましょう。Be 動詞の使い方に注意しながら考えてみてください。冒頭は大文字で書き始め、答えは解答用紙に記入しましょう。

（1）そのイベントの正確な日時については、聞いていません。
［ of the event, the exact, we weren't, date and time, told about ］.
（2）どこで電車を降りるか、忘れないように。
［ where, the train, you, get off, be careful ］.

(3) 次の会議は、来週の金曜日です。
[will be,　meeting,　next Friday,　the next].
(4) もうそれ以上は進まないほうがいいと思うよ。
[recommend,　any further,　I don't,　you to go].
(5) パーティーに来るのが正確には何人だったか、思い出せない。
[the party,　the exact,　people coming to,　I can't recollect,　number of].

B. 並べ替えたものが合っているどうかを、音声を聴いて確かめてみましょう。間違いがある場合は、自分の答えがなぜ間違いなのかを考えてみましょう。

09 Vocabulary（2）：語彙を増やしましょう。

次の日本語表現の意味に合う英語表現を結びつけてみましょう。選んだ答えの表現を解答欄に書き入れましょう。

1. 経済学	2. 教授	3. 大学構内
4. 食堂	5. 親戚	6. 従兄妹
7. 派手な	8. この間の週末	9. あまり楽しくなさそう

語群　cafeteria, campus, colorful, cousin, economics, last weekend,
not very excited, professor, relative

> Vocabulary（2）の表現を使って、次の日本語を英語にしてみよう。ヒントを参考にしてみましょう。

10 Composition：作った英文は解答用紙に記入しましょう。

(1) この間の週末は、親戚の人たちと一緒に USJ に行った。

(2) 私の幼い従兄妹は、あまり楽しくなさそうだった。

(3) この大学構内には、3 つの食堂がある。 *There is/are 構文を使ってみましょう。

(4) あの派手なジャケットを着た男性が、経済学の教授ですか？

11 Exercise：次の（1）から（3）について考えてみましょう。

(1) 過去 1 週間の自分のスケジュールを振り返って、一番忙しかったのはどの日だったか英語で表現してみましょう。本文の内容を踏まえて、"last + day of the week" の表現を使うべきかどうかも考えましょう。

(2) 明日から 1 週間の自分のスケジュールの中から、一番楽しみな予定について英語で表現してみましょう。本文の内容を踏まえて、"next + day of the week" の表現を使うべきかどうかも考えましょう。

(3) Be または Don't be で始まる命令文を 3 つ考えてみましょう。

　　①

　　②

　　③

12 Speed Writing／Discussion／Presentation

(1) クラス内で指示された課題について、クラスメートと話し合ってみましょう。

(2) 話し合いの内容をもとにして、指定された時間内に指定された語数以上で自分の考えを書いてみましょう。この Unit で学んだ文法事項を意識して文章を作ってください。それ以外は文法事項にこだわり過ぎず、できる限り多くの英文を気楽に書いてみましょう。

(3) 自分の考えた文章をクラスメートの前で発表してみましょう。

UNIT 6 ▶ Asking Someone About Their Job

00 Grammar：一般動詞の平叙文・疑問文・命令文について

● 一般動詞とは Be 動詞以外の動詞と考えておきましょう。

☞ 平叙文とは情報や事実を伝える文のことです。肯定文も否定文も平叙文です。

- 肯定文：Children play outside. / The girl plays outside.
- 否定文：Children do not play outside. / The girl does not play outside.

  否定文を作る際は主語が複数なら動詞の前に do not を、単数なら does not を置きます。

☞ 疑問文は主語が複数なら do、単数なら does を主語の前に置き文末には疑問符をつけます。

- 疑問詞（who, whose, what, which, where, why, when, how）を使う場合ははじめに置きます。
- 疑問文：Do children play outside in winter? / Does the girl play outside?

  Where do children play? / Where does the girl play?

☞ 命令文は動詞の原形で始めます。Please などを使って柔らかい表現にもできます。

  否定の命令文の場合は、動詞の前に do not/don't を置きます。

- Play outside. / Please play outside. / Play outside, please. / Don't play outside.

01 Vocabulary（1）：語彙を増やしましょう。

A. 音声を聴いて、次の表現の発音を確認しましょう。その後、その意味を知らない場合 は辞書を使って調べましょう。次に全ての語の意味を解答用紙に記入しましょう。

1. common	2. consider	3. disrespectful	4. direct
5. structure	6. correctly	7. impolite	8. unnatural
9. natural	10. social	11. situation	12. attention
13. pronunciation	14. photojournalism	15. teenager	16. compare
17. similar	18. work-related	19. example	20. division

B. 次の表現は A に入っている単語を定義したものです。それぞれどの単語の定義なのかを考えて、このテキストに答えとなる単語を書き込んでみましょう。

定義	答え
1. to examine people or things to see how they are similar and how they are different　*examine：考察・吟味する	
2. existing in nature; not made or caused by humans　*exist：存在する	
3. happening often; existing in large numbers or in many places	
4. in a way that is accurate or true, without any mistakes	

定義	答え
5. the act of listening to, looking at or thinking about something/ somebody carefully　*act：行為	

02 Reading／Listening：文章の大まかな意味をつかんでみましょう。

◎カズコさんは相手の仕事を知りたい時に、どのような質問をすれば失礼にならないかを尋ねました。

> **Is it polite to ask people about their jobs?**
> **How can I ask someone without sounding impolite?**

この質問に対する回答をまずは音声で聴いてみましょう。一回目はテキストの文章に注意を払いながら聴いてみましょう。二回目は音声を聴いて 1 から 8 のカッコに入る表現を考えながら聴き、書き入れてみましょう。

In the United States, asking someone about their job is one of the most（1.　　　）things to do when meeting that person for the（2.　　　）time. But in some other cultures, this question may be considered disrespectful, so be careful.

(a) Although questions such as "What is your job?" and "What are you?" seem like the most direct ways to ask, we do not use them. The questions are structured（3.　　　）but, to Americans, they can sound（4.　　　）and unnatural.

Instead, we have a few ways to ask that sound more natural. When you meet someone in a（5.　　　）situation, and you want to know what kind of work they do, the most common question is this: What do you do? It is a shorter way of asking: What（6.　　　）you do for a living?

Listen to both questions and some answers you might hear. (b) Pay close attention to the pronunciation of "What do you do?" as it usually sounds like "Whaddya do?" when said quickly:

A: What do you do?　　　　　　　　　　　B: I'm a teacher.
B: What do you do for a living?　　　　　B: I work in photojournalism.
A: What do you do?　　　　　　　　　　　B: I run an arts program for teenagers.
B: What do you do for a living?　　　　　B: I'm a musician.

Compare the question "What do you do?" to "What are you doing?" (c) They sound similar, but the second is not work-related. It is asking what the person is doing right now, this minute.

Two other friendly ways to ask some about their work are "What kind of work do you do?" and "What line of work are you in?" You can answer in the same (7.   ), saying something like, "I run an arts program for teenagers" or "I'm a musician."

After the person answers the question, it is a (8.   ) idea to ask one or two more questions. Listen to an example:

A: What do you do for a living?   B: I run an arts program for teenagers.
A: Nice! How long have you been doing that?   B: For about five years now.
A: Where do you work?   B: At the city's arts and culture division.

03 本文中に出てくる「命令文」を探して、下線を引いてみましょう。

04 **Comprehension Questions：**

単語の意味をある程度知った上で文章を見ると、理解度が高まることが実感できたのではないでしょうか。では内容の確認をしてみましょう。

次の各文の内容が本文の内容と一致している場合はＴを、一致していない場合はＦを選び、解答用紙に○をつけましょう。また本文のどの部分を見れば、判断ができるかについても解答用紙に記入しましょう。

(1)	In America, asking someone about their job when meeting that person for the first time is considered disrespectful.
(2)	To Americans, questions such as "What is your job?" can sound impolite.
(3)	Many Americans use the question "What are you?" because it sounds polite.
(4)	The question "What are you doing?" is not work-related.
(5)	"What kind of work do you do?" is a friendly way to ask someone about their work.

05 **Summary**

次の文章は本文の内容をまとめたものです。（　）内に入る表現の最初の文字を書き出してあります。それをヒントに、本文の中から適切な表現を選んで書き入れましょう。

In the US, asking about jobs is very (1. c   ). However, there are ways to do it in a natural and correct way to avoid being (2. d   ). Using the expressions "what do you do?" is considered polite.

06 Translation（1）

本文中の下線部（a）から（c）を日本語に訳してみましょう。訳は解答用紙に書き入れましょう。

07 Translation（2）

次の文中にはこの Unit でこれまでに見てきた表現が含まれています。気をつけながら日本語に訳してみましょう。知らない表現は辞書で調べて、訳は解答用紙に書き入れましょう。

（1）The man always makes rude remarks about the staff.
（2）Do most schools organize social events for the students?
（3）Correctly answer this question for your chance to win a diamond ring!
（4）Many teenagers do not respect their parents nowadays.
（5）Don't make any decisions when you are angry or tired.

■ 休憩

●アメリカでは社交の場で仕事に関連した質問をするのが一般的ですが、出会ってすぐに尋ねると、個人的すぎる質問と考えられることもあります。また、それなりに親しい人や親戚の間でも、給料については尋ねないのが普通なので気をつけましょう。

08 Word Order：

A. 次の〔　〕内の表現を日本語に合うように並べ替えてみましょう。平叙文、疑問文、命令文の組み立て方を意識しながら考えてみてください。冒頭は大文字で書き始め、答えは解答用紙に記入しましょう。

（1）社長はその役員を解任する権限を持っていません。
〔 remove that officer,　does not have,　the president,　the power,　to 〕.
（2）政府は観光事業において重要な役割を果たしていますか。
〔 in tourism,　play an important role,　the government,　does 〕？
（3）私の母と私は、政治に関して同様の見解を持っている。
〔 have,　similar views on,　and I,　politics,　my mother 〕.

（4） インターネット上の否定的なコメントを気にしないでください。
[on the Internet,　the negative,　don't pay attention to,　comments], please.

（5） 私たちの社会を、別の社会と比較してください。
[other societies,　with,　our societies,　compare].　*compare A with B：A と B を比較する

B. 並べ替えたものが合っているどうかを、音声を聴いて確かめてみましょう。間違いがある場合は、自分の答えがなぜ間違いなのかを考えてみましょう。

09　Vocabulary（2）：語彙を増やしましょう。

次の日本語表現の意味に合う英語表現を結びつけてみましょう。選んだ答えの表現を解答欄に書き入れましょう。

1.　～として（の）	2.　ワクチン接種を受ける	3.　客室乗務員
4.　大統領	5.　信頼できない	6.　～はどうですか
7.　～を押し進める	8.　新型コロナウイルス感染症	9.　笑みを浮かべる

 語群　how do you like,　untrustworthy,　COVID-19,　cabin attendant,
give a smile,　president,　get a vaccine,　as,　proceed with

> Vocabulary（2）の表現を使って、次の日本語を英語にしてみよう。ヒントを参考にしてみましょう。

10 Composition：作った英文は解答用紙に記入しましょう。

(1) 新型コロナウイルスのワクチン接種を受けた後、あなたはどこに行きたいですか。
where を冒頭に置きましょう。 新型コロナウイルスという表現を形容詞的に名詞の前に置いてみましょう。

(2) その信頼できない大統領はいつもわざとらしい笑みを浮かべる。 *unnatural を使いましょう。

(3) 客室乗務員としてのあなたの新しい仕事はどうですか。
*〜としてのという部分を最後に持ってきましょう。

(4) どうぞあなたの仕事をどんどん進めてください。 *please で文を始めてみましょう。

11 Exercise：疑似命令文

「命令文 ＋ and / or」の使い方について考えてみましょう。このタイプの命令文は、通例、条件を表します。そのため、please が付くことはありません。

　　命令文, and … .　　（〜しなさい、そうすれば…。）
　　命令文, or … .　　（〜しなさい、そうでなければ…。）

☞次の各文の（　）内の選択肢の中から、適切な方を選んで〇で囲み、文を完成させましょう。

(1) Hurry up, (and / or) you'll miss the train.
　　[＝ If you don't hurry up, …]
(2) Finish your homework, (and / or) I'll take you to a wildlife park.
　　[＝ If you finish your homework, …]
(3) Eat more beans and vegetables, (and / or) you'll stay healthy.
　　[＝ If you eat more beans and vegetables, …]
(4) Come to a classroom early, (and / or) you'll have a chance to make new friends.
　　[＝ If you come to a classroom early, …]

12 Speed Writing／Discussion／Presentation

(1) クラス内で指示された課題について、クラスメートと話し合ってみましょう。

(2) 話し合いの内容をもとにして、指定された時間内に指定された語数以上で自分の考えを書いてみましょう。この Unit で学んだ文法事項を意識して文章を作ってください。それ以外は文法事項にこだわり過ぎず、できる限り多くの英文を気楽に書いてみましょう。

(3) 自分の考えた文章をクラスメートの前で発表してみましょう。

UNIT 7 ▶ Long Johns and Big Wheels

00 Grammar：受動態について

● 「〜される」の意味を表す受動態は、〈be 動詞（ is / am / are ）＋ 過去分詞〉の形をとります。受動態の時制は be 動詞で決まり、過去を表す時には、be 動詞を過去形（ was / were ）で用います。

☞ **能動態** 〈主語 ＋ 動詞 ＋ 目的語〉「〜が…する」

My mother made the curry and rice.（母がそのカレーライスを作った。）

☞ **受動態** 〈主語 ＋ be 動詞 ＋ 過去分詞 ＋ by 〜〉「ーが〜によって…される」

The curry and rice was made by my mother.（カレーライスは母によって作られた。）

☞ **否定文** 〈be 動詞 ＋ not ＋ 過去分詞〉The curry and rice was <u>not</u> made by my mother.

☞ **疑問文** 〈be 動詞 ＋ 主語 ＋ 過去分詞〉<u>Was</u> the curry and rice made by my mother?

01 Vocabulary（1）：語彙を増やしましょう。

A. 音声を聴いて、次の表現の発音を確認しましょう。その後、その意味を知らない場合は辞書を使って調べましょう。次に全ての語句の意味を解答用紙に記入しましょう。

1. look up	2. term	3. soldier	4. invent
5. consider	6. slang	7. fight	8. include
9. military	10. name	11. famous	12. compete
13. note	14. underwear	15. bake	16. treat
17. wheel	18. follow	19. respect	20. pretty

B. 次の表現は A に入っている単語を定義したものです。それぞれどの単語の定義なのかを考えて、このテキストに答えとなる単語を書き込んでみましょう。

定義	答え
1. a member of the army of a country　*army：軍隊	
2. very informal, sometimes offensive language often used by a particular group of people　*offensive：侮辱的な・攻撃的な、*particular：特有の	
3. known about by many people in many places	
4. to take part in a race or contest against others *take part in：参加する、*against：〜に対して	
5. a feeling of admiring someone or what they do *admiring：感服する・称賛する	

Reading／Listening：文章の大まかな意味をつかんでみましょう。

◎ "long johns" という名前の由来について、レイカさんは次のような質問をしました。

> **Why is a sort of men's underwear called "long johns"?**

この質問に対する回答をまずは音声で聴いてみましょう。一回目はテキストの文章に注意を払いながら聴いてみましょう。二回目は音声を聴いて 1 から 8 のカッコに入る表現を考えながら聴き、書き入れてみましょう。

When I looked up the history of the（1.　　　　　）"long johns," I found it was first used in World War II by American soldiers. That got me thinking about other words and phrases the soldiers（2.　　　　）.

(a) Many words that we use today, or are considered slang terms, came from the soldiers in that war.

Long johns

World War II was fought in many areas, including Europe. Because parts of Europe get cold in winter, the U.S. military gave soldiers special under-clothing to（3.　　　　）keep them warm. This under-clothing covered much of the body, even the arms and legs. The soldiers called it "long johns."

Boxing clothes

Long johns are（4.　　　　）to have been named after John L. Sullivan, a（5.　　　　）American boxer in the 19th century. Sullivan wore a similar-looking piece of clothing when he competed in boxing matches.

(b) It is also worth noting that Americans sometimes call long johns "long underwear."

And, in parts of the U.S., people may use the term "long john" when they talk about a kind of baked sweet that looks like a bar. This treat might help you（6.　　　　）warm in cold weather, too.

Big wheel

The U.S. military is one place（7.　　　　）following orders is very important. Soldiers called someone a "Big Wheel" if that person had power over them. Today, we use this term when talking about someone who has the（8.　　　　）of others.

Long Underwear? Johns?

Here is an example of how to use it in a sentence:

(c)*My father's a pretty big wheel down at the factory*.

03 本文中に出てくる「受動態」を探して、下線を引いてみましょう。

04 Comprehension Questions：

単語の意味をある程度知った上で文章を見ると、理解度が高まることが実感でき
たのではないでしょうか。では内容の確認をしてみましょう。

次の各文の内容が本文の内容と一致している場合は T を、一致していない場合は F
を選び、解答用紙に○をつけましょう。また本文のどの部分を見れば、判断ができ
るかについても解答用紙に記入しましょう。

（1）"Long johns" is the word that American soldiers invented during World War II.
（2）It is believed that "long johns" have been named after an American boxer.
（3）A kind of baked sweet that looks like a bar is also called "long underwear."
（4）"Big wheel" is the term to call someone who does not have the respect of others.
（5）When someone is pretty and tall, you call her a "big wheel."

05 Summary

次の文章は本文の内容をまとめたものです。（　）内に入る表現の最初の文字を書き出してありま
す。それをヒントに、本文の中から適切な表現を選んで書き入れましょう。

Many（1. s　　　　）expressions in English were invented by soldiers serving in the
military. Two popular（2. t　　　　）are "long johns" and "big wheel." Long johns refer to
long-underwear worn by soldiers during World War II. Big wheel is an expression to refer to
someone in charge or has power.

06 Translation（1）

本文中の下線部（a）から（c）を日本語に訳してみましょう。訳は解答用紙に書き入れましょう。

07 Translation（2）

次の文中にはこの Unit でこれまでに見てきた表現が含まれています。気をつけながら日本語に訳してみましょう。知らない表現は辞書で調べて、訳は解答用紙に書き入れましょう。

(1) The weather should be considered for the event.

(2) Breakfast is included in the room rate.

(3) The Tohoku region was damaged badly by the earthquake.

(4) He is pretty tall and looks like a model.

(5) Exercising everyday will help you stay young.

■ 休憩

●受動態では、次の例のように by 以外の前置詞が使われる場合も多くあります。
☞ The ground is covered with snow.　地面は雪で覆われている。
☞ The singer is known to everyone.　その歌手はみんなに知られている。
●また、you, we, they, people など、一般的な人々をさす場合や言う必要がない場合には by～は省略されることがあります。
☞ English is spoken in many countries.　英語は多くの国で話されている。

08 Word Order：

A. 次の ［ ］ 内の表現を日本語に合うように並べ替えてみましょう。受動態の作り方を意識しながら考えてみてください。冒頭は大文字で書き始め、答えは解答用紙に記入しましょう。

(1) 7は幸運の番号だと信じられています。
[a lucky number, to be, seven, believed, is].

(2) 私はここに10時までに来るように言われました。
[come here, was, by 10 o'clock, I, told to].

(3) このかばんは、イタリア製です。
[Italy, made, this bag, is, in].

(4) お金が誰かに盗まれた。
[someone, the money, stolen, by, was].
(5) 誰が日曜日のパーティーに招待されていますか？
[who, invited to, is, on Sunday, the party,]?

B. 並べ替えたものが合っているどうかを、音声を聴いて確かめてみましょう。間違いがある場合
　　は、自分の答えがなぜ間違いなのかを考えてみましょう。

09 **Vocabulary（2）：語彙を増やしましょう。**

次の日本語表現の意味に合う英語表現を結びつけてみましょう。選んだ答えの表現を解答欄に書き
入れましょう。

1. 課題	2. 閉まる	3. 提出する
4. ～に驚く	5. レストラン	6. ～のため
7. 卒業	8. 世界的流行の病	9. 中止する

 語 群　cancel, turn in, be surprised at, assignment, close, graduation, pandemic,
restaurant, due to

> Vocabulary（2）の表現を使って、次の日本語を英語
> にしてみよう。ヒントを参考にしてみましょう。

10 **Composition：作った英文は解答用紙に記入しましょう。**

(1) そのレストランは 7 時に閉店します。 *will を受動態の前に置いてみましょう。
(2) 課題はオンラインで提出されなければいけません。 *turn in を使ってみましょう。
(3) 私はそのニュースにとても驚いた。 *be surprised at～ を使ってみましょう。

(4) 卒業パーティーは世界的流行の病のため中止になった。 *pandemic を使ってみましょう。

11 **Exercise：次の各組の英文がほぼ同じ意味になるように、（　）の中に適語を入れましょう。**

(1) My father turned off the TV.	
= The TV （　　　　　）（　　　　　）（　　　　　　　） by my father.	
(2) I must finish my homework today.	
= The homework （　　　　　）（　　　　　）（　　　　　） today.	
(3) They will sell the tickets to the concert online.	
= The tickets to the concert （　　　　　）（　　　　　）（　　　　　） online.	
(4) My boyfriend gave me this necklace for my birthday.	
= I （　　　　　）（　　　　　） this necklace for my birthday （　　　　） my boyfriend.	

12 **Speed Writing／Discussion／Presentation**

(1) クラス内で指示された課題について、クラスメートと話し合ってみましょう。

(2) 話し合いの内容をもとにして、指定された時間内に指定された語数以上で自分の考えを書いてみましょう。この Unit で学んだ文法事項を意識して文章を作ってください。それ以外は文法事項にこだわり過ぎず、できる限り多くの英文を気楽に書いてみましょう。

(3) 自分の考えた文章をクラスメートの前で発表してみましょう。

UNIT 8 ▶ How Do I Improve My English?

00 Grammar：助動詞（法助動詞）について

● 助動詞は、動詞に意味を付け加える品詞です。法助動詞という表現の「法」とは、話者が発話に関して、どのように捉えているかという「気持ち」を表しています。「法助動詞」を動詞と共に用いると話者の「気持ち」を付け足すことができます。まずは 法助動詞 can と will について、法助動詞ありとなしの文の意味を考えてみましょう。

☞ 法助動詞なしの文：

（1）I speak three languages.　私は 3 ヶ国を話す

☞ can：「～できる」「あり得る」などの可能性を示します。

（2）I can speak three languages.　私は 3 ヶ国を話せる

☞ will：「きっと～する」「～するつもりだ」など確実な未来、意思、決意などを示します。

（3）I will speak three languages.　私はきっと 3 ヶ国を話す！

●（1）の文では単に事実（3 ヶ国を話す）だけを述べています。（2）と（3）には、「話せる（んだよ）」や「きっと話す！」などの話者の気持ちがこめられています。

● 法助動詞のあとには<u>動詞の原形</u>が入ることをおぼえておきましょう。

01 Vocabulary（1）：語彙を増やしましょう。

A. 音声を聴いて、次の表現の発音を確認しましょう。その後、その意味を知らない場合は辞書を使って調べましょう。次に全ての語句の意味を解答用紙に記入しましょう。 **23**

1.　improve	2.　skill	3.　quiet	4.　stay up
5.　in person	6.　set	7.　goal	8.　step
9.　choose	10.　late	11.　important	12.　example
13.　idiom	14.　practice	15.　dinner time	16.　sentence
17.　early	18.　same	19.　get better	20.　together

B. 次の表現は A に入っている単語を定義したものです。それぞれどの単語の定義なのかを考えて、このテキストに答えとなる単語を書き込んでみましょう。

定義	答え
1.　an expression that cannot be understood from the meanings of its separate words, but has a separate meaning of its own *expression：表現、*separate：個々の	
2.　to repeatedly do something in order to become better at it *repeatedly：繰り返して	

定義	答え
3. a group of words that usually contains a subject and a verb, and expresses a complete idea. *contain：含む、*subject：主語、*verb：動詞、*complete：完全な	
4. to make something better, or to become better	
5. having a great effect on people or things; of great value *effect：効果、*value：価値	

02 **Reading／Listening：文章の大まかな意味をつかんでみましょう。**

◎「英語を上達する方法」について、ノリコさんは次のような質問をしました。

Hello!
I want to get better at speaking English and improve my listening skills.
How do I improve my English?

この質問に対する回答をまずは音声で聴いてみましょう。一回目はテキストの文章に注意を払いながら聴いてみましょう。二回目は音声を聴いて 1 から 8 のカッコに入る表現を考えながら聴き、書き入れてみましょう。

Study at the same time each day

The first step in getting better in English is to study at the （1.　　　　）time each day. (a)Do you wake up early and study when the house is quiet? Or do you like to stay up （2.　　　　）and study before you go to sleep? Choose a time to study English （3.　　　　）or every week. Make a study plan for each week.

Find a friend to study together

A good way to learn is to study with a （4.　　　　）or a family member. You can study （5.　　　　）in person or on the phone. Some families speak English （6.　　　　）at dinner time or watch English videos together.

Set a goal

One of the most important steps to learn English is to set a goal. (b)Make it something you know you *can* do in a short time. Here are some examples:

- I will learn four new **idioms** in the next month and use them with friends.

- I will practice speaking with my friends three times (7.   ).
- (c)I will write sentences with five new English words every week.

Start with these (8.   ): study at the same time, study with a friend and set a goal.

03 本文中に出てくる「法助動詞」を探して、下線を引いてみましょう。

04 Comprehension Questions：

> 単語の意味をある程度知った上で文章を見ると、理解度が高まることが実感できたのではないでしょうか。では内容の確認をしてみましょう。

次の各文の内容が本文の内容と一致している場合はTを、一致していない場合はFを選び、解答用紙に〇をつけましょう。また本文のどの部分を見れば、判断ができるかについても解答用紙に記入しましょう。

（1）It is important to study English at the same place every day.
（2）It is a good idea to study with your friends and family.
（3）Making specific plans for your study helps you improve your English.
（4）It is a good idea to set goals you can achieve in a short time.
（5）One way to practice speaking English is to listen to English songs at dinner time.

05 Summary

次の文章は本文の内容をまとめたものです。（　）内に入る表現の最初の文字を書き出してあります。それをヒントに、本文の中から適切な表現を選んで書き入れましょう。

There are 3 steps to（1. i   ）your English skills. The first step is to study at the same time each day. The second is to find a friend or family member to study with, together. One tip is to study together as a family during dinner by speaking（2. o   ）English. Finally, the third is to have a goal you can reach. For example, practicing with your friends or learning new words.

06 Translation（1）

本文中の下線部（a）から（c）を日本語に訳してみましょう。訳は解答用紙に書き入れましょう。

Translation（2）

次の文中にはこの Unit でこれまでに見てきた表現が含まれています。気をつけながら日本語に訳してみましょう。知らない表現は辞書で調べて、訳は解答用紙に書き入れましょう。

（1） I want to get better at cooking various dishes.
（2） I'll stay up all night, if necessary, to finish the project.
（3） Let's discuss the issue either on the phone or in person.
（4） I will learn to cook one new dish every week.
（5） We must take bold steps to protect the environment.

■ **休憩**

●will と can の否定の形について考えてみましょう。will の否定 will not ＝ won't は「必ず～しない」と拒絶を意味します。can の否定 cannot ＝ can't は「できない、ありえない、～のはずがない」という意味になります。
　☞ My friend won't listen to my advice.　友人が私のアドバイスを聞こうとしない。
　☞ The news can't be true.　そのニュースが本当のはずがない。
●その他の法助動詞（may. should, must）についても考えてみましょう。
　☞ may：「～してもよい」「～かもしれない」という意味。
　　（1） The news may be true.　そのニュースは本当かもしれない
　☞ should「～するべき」「本来ならば～するのが当然」」という意味。
　　（2） You should stay home.　あなたは家にいる方がいいですよ。
　　（3） The news should be true.　そのニュースは本当のはずだ。
　☞ must「～しなければならない」「～に違いない」という意味。
　　（4） We must stay home.　我々は家にいなければならない。
　　（5） The news must be true.　そのニュースは本当に違いない。

Word Order：

A. 次の ［　］ 内の表現を日本語に合うように並べ替えてみましょう。助動詞をどこに置けばいいかを意識しながら考えてみてください。冒頭は大文字で書き始め、答えは解答用紙に記入しましょう。

（1） 私は来週必ず友人と英語を話す練習をする。
［ practice,　with my friends,　speaking,　I will,　next week,　English ］.

(2) あなたは私と直接会って話すことができます。
[person, you, in, talk to me, can].
(3) 晩ご飯の時に、スペイン語のみを話す家族もいる。
[at dinner time, only Spanish, speak, some families].
(4) 私は今日から毎日必ず、新しい5つの英単語を用いて文を書きます。
[with five new words, I will, every day, starting today, write sentences].
(5) 私はそれを、短い時間内で行うことができる。
[it, I, do , can, in a short time].

B. 並べ替えたものが合っているどうかを、音声を聴いて確かめてみましょう。間違いがある場合は、自分の答えがなぜ間違いなのかを考えてみましょう。

09 Vocabulary（2）：語彙を増やしましょう。

次の日本語表現の意味に合う英語表現を結びつけてみましょう。選んだ答えの表現を解答欄に書き入れましょう。

1. 近いうちに	2. 話し合う	3. 全く〜ない
4. 開く	5. 直接（会って）	6. 〜していただけますか
7. 旅行の予定	8. 約束する	9. 貸す

 語 群　in person, plans for the trip, soon, not~ at all, promise, lend, will you, discuss, open

> Vocabulary（2）の表現を使って、次の日本語を英語にしてみよう。ヒントを参考にしてみましょう。

10 Composition：作った英文は解答用紙に記入しましょう。

（1）お金を貸していただけますか？

（2）ドアが全く開かない。

（3）私はあなたの誕生日に必ず何か買うと約束します。

（4）私たちは近いうちに直接会って、旅行の予定について話し合えます。

11 Exercise：以下の 4 つの文に法助動詞（can, will, must, should, may）のいずれかを加えて、可能（〜することができる）、推測（〜だろう）、義務（〜しなければならない、〜するべきだ）、推量（〜かもしれない）などの意味を表す文に変えてみましょう。また必要に応じて、"next month," "in summer," "in my hometown" などの表現も加えてみましょう。

例）The news is true. →　The news <u>may</u> be true.
そのニュースは真実です　そのニュースは真実かもしれない

（1）I always maintain a healthy, balanced diet.　＊diet：食事

（2）There is a powerful storm.

（3）It rains a lot.

（4）Traveling becomes easier and easier.

12 Speed Writing／Discussion／Presentation

（1）クラス内で指示された課題について、クラスメートと話し合ってみましょう。

（2）話し合いの内容をもとにして、指定された時間内に指定された語数以上で自分の考えを書いてみましょう。この Unit で学んだ文法事項を意識して文章を作ってください。それ以外は文法事項にこだわり過ぎず、できる限り多くの英文を気楽に書いてみましょう。

（3）自分の考えた文章をクラスメートの前で発表してみましょう。

UNIT 9 ▶▶ Silent Letters

00 Grammar：動名詞、不定詞（名詞的用法）について

●動詞は動作などを表すことばです（「寝る」など）。一方、名詞は物などを表します（「ラーメン」など）。文中で名詞を使うところに、動詞をそのまま入れることはできません。
　☞ ○：「私は<u>ラーメン</u>が好きです。」
　☞ ×：「私は<u>寝る</u>が好きです。」
●これは英語でも同じです。名詞を使うところに動詞を使う場合、日本語では、「～する<u>こと</u>」「～する<u>の</u>」という形を使います。（「私は寝る<u>の</u>が好きです。」）英語でこれにあたるのが、動名詞と名詞的用法の不定詞です。動名詞は動詞に -ing をつけます。不定詞は、動詞の前に to をつけます。
　☞ ○：I like <u>ramen</u>.［名詞］
　☞ ×：I like <u>sleep</u>.［そのままの動詞］
　☞ ○：I like <u>sleeping</u>.［動名詞］/ I like <u>to sleep</u>.［不定詞］

01 Vocabulary（1）：語彙を増やしましょう。

A. 音声を聴いて、次の表現の発音を確認しましょう。その後、その意味を知らない場合は辞書を使って調べましょう。次に全ての語句の意味を解答用紙に記入しましょう。

 26

1. silent	2. letter	3. pronounce	4. history
5. language	6. borrow	7. simplify	8. over time
9. century	10. spelling	11. sound	12. separate
13. Middle English	14. come along	15. vowel	16. another
17. Greek	18. German	19. Old English	20. different

B. 次の表現は A に入っている単語を定義したものです。それぞれどの単語の定義なのかを考えて、このテキストに答えとなる単語を書き込んでみましょう。

定義	答え
1. to appear or occur	
2. make something easier	
3. without any sound	
4. to take or copy someone's ideas, words etc. and use them in your own work, language etc.	
5. a period of 100 years	

02 **Reading／Listening：文章の大まかな意味をつかんでみましょう。**

◎英語の単語のつづりと発音について、リカさんは次のような質問をしました。

> Hello! Why do we have some silent letters in English? Like these words: write, know, half, hide. So, tell me, why should we write them, although we don't pronounce them?

この質問に対する回答をまずは音声で聴いてみましょう。一回目はテキストの文章に注意を払いながら聴いてみましょう。二回目は音声を聴いて 1 から 8 のカッコに入る表現を考えながら聴き、書き入れてみましょう。

Like many of the unusual things about English, the answer is tied to (1.　　　　). Three of the reasons for the silent letters are changes in the language, borrowing words or terms from other languages and simplification of words.

If you pay close attention, you will find my answer to your second question: "Why should we write them?"

The first (2.　　　　) is that language changes over time, and as people move from place to place. The English language has been written for over 10 centuries. We all know the way speakers of English pronounce words has changed over the years. However, the (3.　　　　) of many of those words has not changed.

(a) About 400 years ago, people said the "w" sound or /w/ at the beginning of your first example, "write." In the Northeast of Scotland, you may still (4.　　　　) the sound "v" at the beginning of the word.

You asked about the word "hide." That has a silent "e" because at one time, there were two syllables or separate parts to the word. In (5.　　　　) English, one might say /heed-uh/. This word was part of a big change in the way people speak English. It came along between the years 1400 and 1700 and is called the Great Vowel Shift. The vowels – sounds you make with an open mouth – began to change. /Heed-uh/ became "hide." After that change, English speakers kept writing words with the silent "e" to show that the words have a long vowel sound within the word.

Another reason for silent letters is that English has borrowed words from many other languages. Words that came from Greek may (6.　　　　) with the letters "ph", but we say them with a "f" sound, /f/ as in "physical." (b) Scholars decided to write them

— 50

in the Greek way to show their roots.

You can imagine that people want to make the language they speak simpler. That is true with pronunciation, but until today, there have been few major changes to the spelling of English words. Two centuries ago, Noah Webster tried to change American spelling in his dictionary. He is the reason Americans spell "color" without the letter "u" and spell "jail" as j-a-i-l, not "g-a-o-l."

The second word you asked about – "know" – came from an old German word. In (7.   ) English and in old German, the "k" sound was heard at the beginning. But to make it simpler, people started to say the "n" at the beginning. (c)Today, we write the word "know" as "k-n-o-w" to show that it is different from the word spelled n-o, or "no." The same is (8.   ) for all other words that begin with the letters "kn."

03 本文中に出てくる「動名詞」「名詞的用法の不定詞」を探して、下線を引いてみましょう。

04 Comprehension Questions：

単語の意味をある程度知った上で文章を見ると、理解度が高まることが実感できたのではないでしょうか。では内容の確認をしてみましょう。

次の各文の内容が本文の内容と一致している場合はTを、一致していない場合はFを選び、解答用紙に○をつけましょう。また本文のどの部分を見れば、判断ができるかについても解答用紙に記入しましょう。

| （1） Writing English words started more than 1000 years ago. |
| （2） The spelling of all English words has changed over the years. |
| （3） Between the years 1400 and 1700, there was a big change in the way people spoke English. |
| （4） People want to make the pronunciation of the language they speak simpler. |
| （5） The word "know" came from an old Greek word. |

05 Summary

次の文章は本文の内容をまとめたものです。（　　）内に入る表現の最初の文字を書き出してあります。それをヒントに、本文の中から適切な表現を選んで書き入れましょう。

The strange spelling of some English words is because of their (1. h　　　　). There are a few reasons for (2. s　　　　) letters. One is that the language and spelling has changed over time and because people move, so pronunciation often changes but the way words are written did not. Another reason is the Great Vowel Shift between 1400-1700. Other reasons include borrowed words from Greek, like words that start with "ph" or German and Old English words that start with "kn."

06 Translation（1）

本文中の下線部（a）から（c）を日本語に訳してみましょう。訳は解答用紙に書き入れましょう。

07 Translation（2）

次の文中にはこの Unit でこれまでに見てきた表現が含まれています。気をつけながら日本語に訳してみましょう。知らない表現は辞書で調べて、訳は解答用紙に書き入れましょう。

（1）That concert was so exciting that we couldn't sleep. We kept talking about it all night. ＊so～that ... :「とても～なので…」という意味。
（2）There are 26 letters in the alphabet.
（3）She wanted to be an actress, so she decided to go to Tokyo after graduating high school.
（4）Japanese has borrowed many words from other languages.
（5）Understanding the change of public opinion over time is especially helpful in tracking the political effects of the act.＊Under standing から over time までがこの文の主部。＊tracking the political effects of the act:「この法案の政治的な効果（の変遷）をたどること」

■ 休憩 ┈┈

●日本語の「～すること」「～するの」にあたる英語は、動名詞と名詞的用法の不定詞ですが、どちらを使えるかが決まっている場合があります。Keep（［～すること］を続ける）の後ろには動名詞、decide（［～すること］を決心する）の後ろには名詞的用法の不定詞を使います。
　　☞ ○ : He decided to join the team.
　　☞ × : He decided joining the team.
　　　　　彼はそのチームに入ることを決心した。

08 Word Order：

A. 次の ［　］内の表現を日本語に合うように並べ替えてみましょう。動名詞、不定詞に 注意しながら考えてみてください。冒頭は大文字で書き始め、答えは解答用紙に記入しましょう。

（1） ジョンと彼女との関係は、時間がたっても変わっていない。
［ John and his girlfriend，has not，the relationship，changed over time，between ］.
（2） その戦争が起きた第一の理由は、王が息子のないまま死んだことだ。
［ reason for the war，is that，the first，the king，died without sons ］.
（3） 私は、お金をためてヨーロッパに行きたい。
［ to Europe，and go，I，to save money，want ］.
（4） ボブは、壊れたコンピューターを自分で直そうとした。
［ fix，tried，his broken computer by himself，Bob，to ］.
（5） 彼は俳優になりたくて、何年もオーディションを受け続けた。
［ he，to be，auditioning for years，an actor and kept，wanted ］.

B. 並べ替えたものが合っているどうかを、音声を聴いて確かめてみましょう。間違いがある場合は、自分の答えがなぜ間違いなのかを考えてみましょう。

09 Vocabulary（2）：語彙を増やしましょう。

次の日本語表現の意味に合う英語表現を結びつけてみましょう。選んだ答えの表現を解答欄に書き入れましょう。

1. 決心する	2. 友達	3. ～に（電子）メールを送る
4. 続ける	5. 個人情報	6. 掲示する
7. 避ける	8. ～について	9. 話す

語群　avoid，keep，about，email，friend，talk，post，personal information，decide

10 Composition：作った英文は解答用紙に記入しましょう。

（1）彼は、スペインに行ってサッカーをすることを決心した。

（2）彼女は、アメリカにいる友達にメールを送り続けた。　*keep の過去形 kept を使ってみましょう。

（3）自分の個人情報をインターネットに掲示することは避けましょう。

（4）私は友達と音楽について話すのが好きだ。

11 Exercise：次の（1）と（2）について考えてみましょう。

（1）この章で学んだ、「動名詞」「名詞的用法の不定詞」を含む構文を使って、自分のことを英語
　　で表現してみましょう。分からない語句は辞書で調べましょう。

　　①私は、将来〜すると決めている。I have decided to _____ ... in the future.

　　②私は、〜したい。I want to _____ ... .

　　③私は、〜するのが好きだ。I like to _____ ... . / I like _____ -ing ... .

　　④私は、〜することを続けている。I keep _____ -ing ... .

　　⑤私は、〜することを避けている。I avoid _____ ing ... .

（2）上の構文を使った英文を、インターネットで探してみましょう。

12 Speed Writing／Discussion／Presentation

（1）クラス内で指示された課題について、クラスメートと話し合ってみましょう。

（2）話し合いの内容をもとにして、指定された時間内に指定された語数以上で自分の考えを書い
　　てみましょう。この Unit で学んだ文法事項を意識して文章を作ってください。それ以外は文
　　法事項にこだわり過ぎず、できる限り多くの英文を気楽に書いてみましょう。

（3）自分の考えた文章をクラスメートの前で発表してみましょう。

UNIT 10 ▶ Anything and Nothing

00 Grammar：不定詞（形容詞的用法・副詞的用法）について

●不定詞は、主語の人称や数によって限定されることなく、「to＋動詞の原型」という形で、Unit 9 で学んだような「名詞的」な働きに加えて、「形容詞的」な働きや「副詞的」な働きをします。

☞（1）She has a lot of books to read.　彼女は読むべきたくさんの本を持っている。

☞（2）The dogs ran down the stairs to play outside.　犬たちは外で遊ぶために階段を駆け下りた。

●（1）の下線部分は "books" の後ろに置かれ、「読むべき」という意味で "books" を修飾しているので「形容詞的用法」と言います。

●（2）の下線部分は直前の名詞 "stairs" を修飾しているわけではなく、文意から「遊ぶために」と目的を述べていることがわかります。これは「副詞的用法」と呼ばれます。

01 Vocabulary（1）：語彙を増やしましょう。

A. 音声を聴いて、次の表現の発音を確認しましょう。その後、その意味を知らない場合は辞書を使って調べましょう。次に全ての語の意味を解答用紙に記入しましょう。

1. mind	2. express	3. kind	4. negative
5. statement	6. example	7. remember	8. way
9. mail	10. add	11. form	12. absence
13. lack	14. person	15. verb	16. appear
17. singular	18. apply	19. rule	20. create

B. 次の表現は A に入っている単語を定義したものです。それぞれどの単語の定義なのかを考えて、このテキストに答えとなる単語を書き込んでみましょう。

定義	答え
1. a group of people or things having similar characteristics *characteristic：特質・特徴	
2. a method, style, or manner of doing something　*method：方法	
3. to put something together with something else so as to increase the size, number, amount, etc.　*increase：大きくする、*amount：量	
4. the state of being away from a place or person　*state：状態・状況	
5. to make a formal application or request　*application：申し込み	

◎ "anything and nothing" の使い方について、チヨさんは次のような質問をしました。

> I would like to know tips on how to choose affirmative or negative sentences while using 'nothing', 'no one' or 'nobody', or 'anything,' 'anyone' or 'anybody'.

この質問に対する回答をまずは音声で聴いてみましょう。一回目はテキストの文章に注意を払いながら聴いてみましょう。二回目は音声を聴いて 1 から 8 のカッコに入る表現を考えながら聴き、書き入れてみましょう。

Anything, anyone, anybody

With that in mind, we see that "anything" is a word English speakers use to（1.　　　　　　）"a thing of any kind" in a question or a negative statement. Here are（2.　　　　　　）of both:

> *Do they have anything to eat?*
> *They do not have anything to eat.*

(a)Remember, the negative statement can only have one negative, and, here, it is the word "not." This works the same（3.　　　　　　）with the other words you asked about, "anyone" and "anybody." For example,

> *Has anyone come to pick up the mail today?*
> *I have not seen anyone this morning.*

The negative answer uses "not" and "anyone." (b)You can also add "never" to make a negative statement, as in:

> *They never found anybody to do that job.*

Nothing, no one and nobody

Now, let us look at the negative（4.　　　　　　）, "nothing," "nobody" and "no one." We use these to talk about an（5.　　　　　　）or lack of a thing or a person. The（6.　　　　　　）form that appears with these words is always（7.　　　　　　）because you cannot have more than one of nothing! (c)Starting with "nothing," you can apply our rule again to create a statement with only one negative. Here is how we can use anything and nothing together.

> *Is anything happening at your school today?*
> *There is nothing happening at school. Today is*

> Do you have anything to play with?

> There is nothing to disturb me.

a (8.   ).

We can use "nobody" in the same way: in answer to a question that uses "anybody."

Did anybody help you write the letter?
Nobody helped me. I did it all by myself.

03 本文中に出てくる「不定詞（形容詞的用法と副詞的用法）」を探して、下線を引いてみましょう。

04 **Comprehension Questions：**

単語の意味をある程度知った上で文章を見ると、理解度が高まることが実感できたのではないでしょうか。では内容の確認をしてみましょう。

次の各文の内容が本文の内容と一致している場合はＴを、一致していない場合はＦを選び、解答用紙に〇をつけましょう。また本文のどの部分を見れば、判断ができるかについても解答用紙に記入しましょう。

（1）"Something" is a word English speakers use to express "a thing of any kind" in a question.
（2）The verb form that appears with "nothing" is always singular.
（3）The negative statement can have two negative words.
（4）You can create a negative statement with "not" and "anyone."
（5）You can say, "I do not have nothing to eat."

05 **Summary**

次の文章は本文の内容をまとめたものです。（　）内に入る表現の最初の文字を書き出してあります。それをヒントに、本文の中から適切な表現を選んで書き入れましょう。

Using the expressions: anything, anyone, anybody and nothing, no one and nobody can be challenging. The words with "any' in them are often found in examples of questions or （1. n   ） statements to express "a thing of any kind." Nothing, no one, and nobody are negative forms that explain （2. a   ） or lack.

06 **Translation（1）**

本文中の下線部（a）から（c）を日本語に訳してみましょう。訳は解答用紙に書き入れましょう。

07 Translation（2）

次の文中にはこの Unit でこれまでに見てきた表現が含まれています。気をつけながら日本語に訳してみましょう。知らない表現は辞書で調べて、訳は解答用紙に書き入れましょう。

（1） Do you have anything to drink?
（2） As you know, there is no rule to follow.
（3） There is nothing to worry about.
（4） You can't take anyone to help you with the work.
（5） Here is how we can use the verb to create a sentence.

■ 休憩 ‑‑‑

●「副詞的用法」では「目的」以外に、「結果」「原因」「判断の根拠」「条件」などを表す場合もあります。文脈で判断しましょう。
　☞（1）She grew up to be a famous artist.
　　　彼女は大きくなって有名な芸術家になりました。：「結果」
　☞（2）I am glad to hear that.
　　　それを聞いて嬉しい。：「原因」
　☞（3）You are very kind to show me the way.
　　　道を教えてくれるなんて、とても親切ですね。：「判断の根拠」
　☞（4）To hear her talk, you would think she is an American.
　　　彼女が話すのを聞いたら、彼女がアメリカ人だと思うだろう。「条件」

08 Word Order：

A. 次の ［　］ 内の表現を日本語に合うように並べ替えてみましょう。不定詞をどこに置けばいいかを意識しながら考えてみてください。冒頭は大文字で書き始め、答えは解答用紙に記入しましょう。

（1） 誰かあなたを迎えに来ましたか。
［ anyone,　pick you up,　come,　to,　did ］?
（2） 彼女は料理を美味しくするものを何も加えなかった。
［ she added,　the dish,　tasty,　nothing,　to make ］.

(3) レポートを書くのに、そのコンピュータが使えますよ。

[you can, a paper, write, use the computer, to].

(4) 手伝ってくれる人を連れてきませんでした。

[anyone, I never, to, brought, help me].

(5) 守るべき交通規則について見てみましょう。

[obey, look at, let us, to, the traffic rules].

B. 並べ替えたものが合っているどうかを、音声を聴いて確かめてみましょう。間違いがある場合は、自分の答えがなぜ間違いなのかを考えてみましょう。

09 Vocabulary（2）：語彙を増やしましょう。

次の日本語表現の意味に合う英語表現を結びつけてみましょう。選んだ答えの表現を解答欄に書き入れましょう。

1. 週末	2. 提出する	3. 課題
4. 報告する	5. 頭痛	6. 図書館
7. 試験	8.（苦痛などを）緩和する	9. 薬

語群　library, submit, report, examination, medicine, assignment, relieve, weekend, headache

> Vocabulary（2）の表現を使って、次の日本語を英語にしてみよう。ヒントを参考にしてみましょう。

10 Composition：作った英文は解答用紙に記入しましょう。

---

(1) 私は今週末までに提出する課題があります。 *by を使ってみましょう。

---

(2) 皆さんに報告することがあります。 *I have ～で表現してみましょう。

---

(3) 彼女は試験勉強をするために図書館に行きました。 *study for～ を使ってみましょう。

---

(4) 頭痛に効く薬はありますか。 *Do you have ～ ? で表現してみましょう。

---

11 Exercise：この Unit で勉強した代名詞（anything, anyone, anybody, nothing, no one, nobody）や不定詞（形容詞用法・副詞的用法）を実際に使って話してみましょう！以下の状況において、英語で何と言えばよいでしょうか。相手に話しかけるつもりで、英語で話してみましょう。

(1) 退屈そうな妹。あなたは、何もすることがないのか妹に尋ねたい。

　　→ Don't you have ＿＿＿＿＿＿＿ ?

(2) 寒い日なのに薄着の友達。何か着るものを持っていないのか尋ねたい。

　　→ Don't you have ＿＿＿＿＿＿＿＿ ?

(3) あなたは本を買いに書店に出かけていた。帰宅後、どこに行っていたのかと尋ねられたことに対して説明する。

　　→ I went to ＿＿＿＿＿＿＿＿＿ .

(4) 食べ物を欲しがる鳩に囲まれるあなた。あげるものがないことを鳩につぶやきたい。

　　→ Sorry, but I have ＿＿＿＿＿＿＿＿ .

12 Speed Writing／Discussion／Presentation

(1) クラス内で指示された課題について、クラスメートと話し合ってみましょう。

(2) 話し合いの内容をもとにして、指定された時間内に指定された語数以上で自分の考えを書いてみましょう。この Unit で学んだ文法事項を意識して文章を作ってください。それ以外は文法事項にこだわり過ぎず、できる限り多くの英文を気楽に書いてみましょう。

(3) 自分の考えた文章をクラスメートの前で発表してみましょう。

UNIT 11 ▶ All About "Develop"

00 Grammar：動詞で表わす「時」

●文が表す出来事は①現在、②過去、③未来という3つの基本的な「時」のいずれかによって区別されます。それぞれの「時」を表すためには動詞を適切な形に変化させる必要があります。下線部の語句の形に注意しましょう。

☞(1) The pie <u>smells</u> delicious. 　　　そのパイはおいしそうな匂いだ。　　[現在]

☞(2) My mother <u>baked</u> an apple pie. 　お母さんがりんごパイを焼いた。　　[過去]

☞(3) The party <u>will start</u> at five p.m. 　パーティーは午後5時にはじまる。　[未来]

●(1) では現在形を用いて現在（＝この文を述べているとき）の状況を表しています。

●(2) が過去の出来事であることは動詞の語尾に -d がついていることからわかります。

●(3) では未来に起こる事を表すために will と動詞の原形という2つの語を組み合わせた形が使われています。

01 Vocabulary（1）：語彙を増やしましょう。

A．音声を聴いて、次の表現の発音を確認しましょう。その後、その意味を知らない場合は辞書を使って調べましょう。次に全ての語の意味を解答用紙に記入しましょう。

1. grow	2. skill	3. create	4. recent
5. industry	6. medical	7. symptom	8. identify
9. disease	10. fever	11. award	12. product
13. process	14. describe	15. income	16. usage
17. expert	18. affect	19. mental	20. physical

B．次の表現は A に入っている単語を定義したものです。それぞれどの単語の定義なのかを考えて、このテキストに答えとなる単語を書き込んでみましょう。

定義	答え
1. show what someone or something is like	
2. cause something to happen or exist	
3. a person who knows a lot about a special subject	
4. the making or production of things in factories	
5. a prize or certificate that a person is given for doing something well	

◎マサコさんの質問に対して、先生はここで "Develop" が表す様々な意味について説明しています。

Hi. Could you explain more about the meanings of the word "Develop" with examples?

この質問に対する回答をまずは音声で聴いてみましょう。一回目はテキストの文章に注意を払いながら聴いてみましょう。二回目は音声を聴いて１から８のカッコに入る表現を考えながら聴き、書き入れてみましょう。

33

Develop is a verb, or action word. It means to（1.   ）. Here is an example sentence: *Andrew's skill at basketball developed slowly, but now he is the best player on his team.* In other words, Andrew（2.   ）about basketball over time and became a good player. You could say: *Good coaching and a lot of practice helped Andrew develop his ability.*

Develop can also mean（3.   ）. *The teacher developed the new English teaching program and now his students understand prepositions.* Here is an example from a recent Learning English news story: *Countries in the area are trying to develop their own steel or aluminum industries.* (a)In other words, the countries do not have steel or aluminum industries now. They are working to create these industries.

Develop is also often used in the language of the medical world. A doctor might ask you: *When did your symptoms develop?* (b)She is trying to find out when your sickness began. This can help her identify what（4.   ）or condition you have.

The noun form of develop is development. Let's say you answered the doctor's question about your symptoms. The doctor might write in her notes: *Patient began coughing four days ago. The development of*（5.   ）*is unknown.* Here is another example. Imagine your good friend got an award at his new job. You might say: *Congratulations! That is a promising development. Maybe you will get a pay raise!* And in the business world, you will often hear: *The product is in development.* That means the product is in the（6.   ）of creation. It is not ready to market yet.

There are also adjectival and adverbial forms of develop. (c)For example, we often describe middle- to low-income countries as developing nations. "Developing" in that（7.   ）is an adjective.

develop

The adverb for "develop" is made from the noun development. Listen: *The man is developmentally disabled*. Medical（8.　　　　　）say this means a person is severely affected by a problem with mental ability, physical ability, or both!

03 本文中から過去、現在、未来を表す動詞を探して下線を引きましょう。

04 Comprehension Questions：

単語の意味をある程度知った上で文章を見ると、理解度が高まることが実感できたのではないでしょうか。では内容の確認をしてみましょう。

次の各文の内容が本文の内容と一致している場合はTを、一致していない場合はFを選び、解答用紙に〇をつけましょう。また本文のどの部分を見れば、判断ができるかについても解答用紙に記入しましょう。

（1）The verb "develop" grows slowly into an action verb.
（2）The verb "develop" was created in the industries of steel or aluminum.
（3）A doctor may use the word "develop" when he or she asks patients about their sickness.
（4）If a product is ready to market, it is in development.
（5）There are different forms of "develop" for a noun, an adjective, and an adverb.

05 Summary

次の文章は本文の内容をまとめたものです。（　）内に入る表現の最初の文字を書き出してあります。それをヒントに、本文の中から適切な表現を選んで書き入れましょう。

The word develop has many uses as a verb, an adjective, and even an adverb. It can be used to talk about the improvement or progress of skill. Also, develop can be used in to discuss building or creating new（1.　i　　　　）or in the medical field when discussing and identifying symptoms. Develop can also be used when talking about（2.　i　　　　　）and the wealth of countries.

06 Translation（1）
本文中の下線部（a）から（c）を日本語に訳してみましょう。訳は解答用紙に書き入れましょう。

07 Translation（2）
次の文中にはこの Unit でこれまでに見てきた表現が含まれています。気をつけながら日本語に訳してみましょう。知らない表現は辞書で調べて、訳は解答用紙に書き入れましょう。

(1) It is difficult to say at present how the industry will develop.
(2) My grandmother always grows vegetables in the garden.
(3) The company is creating a whole new drug.
(4) I described exactly how my symptoms had developed.
(5) The developing nation is in the process of building roads across the country.

■ 休憩①

●(1) の文における動詞の現在形は、習慣的に従事していることを表しているのであって、今まさに行われていることを言ってはいません。
　　☞(1) I study English.　私は英語を学んでいます。
●また、実際に成り立つと考えられる条件を表す節では、同じ現在形でも未来を表します。
　　☞ If it rains tomorrow, the school trip will be postponed.
　　　もし明日が雨なら、修学旅行は延期されます。
●英語の動詞には、原形（不定形）、現在形、過去形、分詞形など、いくつかの「形」があり、それぞれが様々な時に関する「意味」と結びついて用いられます。「未来」のように will と原形動詞を組み合わせて表わす場合もあります。このように動詞の形と意味の結びつきは大変複雑で、時制という大きな仕組みの中で見る必要があります。

08 Word Order：

A. 次の [　] 内の表現を日本語に合うように並べ替えてみましょう。動詞とその時制に注意しながら考えてみてください。冒頭は大文字で書き始め、答えは解答用紙に記入しましょう。

(1) 先進諸国は新しいハイテク産業を生み出そうと懸命である。 [trying to develop,　high-tech industries,　developed countries are,　new].
(2) 私はどれが自分の傘か区別がつくように名札をつけた。 [my,　a name tag to,　I attached,　umbrella to identify it].
(3) もし君がこのプロジェクトを成功させたら、賃金があがるよ。 [a pay raise if,　this project a success,　you make,　you will get].
(4) ケンのタイピングの技能は急速に上達し、今や彼はプログラマーだ。 [is,　Ken's skill at typing,　a programmer,　and now he,　developed quickly].

（5）十分な睡眠とたくさんの運動はエイミーの仕事ぶりを向上させるのに役立った。

[helped Amy develop, and a lot of exercise, her performance, enough sleep].

B. 並べ替えたものが合っているどうかを、音声を聴いて確かめてみましょう。間違いがある場合
は、自分の答えがなぜ間違いなのかを考えてみましょう。

09 Vocabulary（2）：語彙を増やしましょう。

次の日本語表現の意味に合う英語表現を結びつけてみましょう。選んだ答えの表現を解答欄に書き
入れましょう。

1. 問題	2. 答え	3. いつもの
4. 叔父	5. 発明する	6. 便利な
7. 文房具	8. 巨大な	9. ショッピングモール

 語 群　uncle, solution, stationery product, problem, shopping mall, invent, usual,
huge, useful

Vocabulary（2）の表現を使って、次の日本語を英語
にしてみよう。ヒントを参考にしてみましょう。

10 Composition：作った英文は解答用紙に記入しましょう。

（1）私はどんな問題にも答えはあると信じている。 *現在の「状態」であることに注意しましょう。

（2）太郎がいつもの席で昼食を食べている。 *いま行われている最中の出来事を述べています。

（3）私の叔父は 1993 年に便利な文房具を発明した。 *stationary product を使ってみましょう。

（4）来年この町に巨大なショッピングモールがオープンします。 *これから起こる事を表します。

■ 休憩②　‥‥‥

●英語には「完了」という時の捉え方があります。Grammar の解説で示した現在・過去・未来のいずれかの時を基準にして「その時までの出来事を振り返る」という意味を表すときに用いられます。
☞（1）現在完了形：現在から振り返る出来事…*have ＋ 過去分詞形*
I have finished my homework.
宿題は終わらせました。
☞（2）過去完了形：過去の時点から振り返る出来事…*had ＋ 過去分詞形*
The film had already begun when we arrived at the theater.
劇場に着いたときにはもう映画は始まっていました。
☞（3）未来完了形：未来の時点から振り返る出来事…
will ＋ have ＋ 過去分詞形
I will have left here before the graduation ceremony.
卒業式を待たずに私はここを発っていることでしょう。

11 Exercise：次の日記には意味の通らないおかしな箇所が 4 つあります。例にならって次の問いに答えましょう。

（1）おかしいと思う箇所に下線を引きましょう。
（2）下線部の何がおかしいか指摘し、下の解答欄に記入しましょう。
（3）意味が通る文にするために、下線部に入る正しい英語を下の解答欄に記入しましょう。

School Trip

I am writing this shortly after I returned from the school trip. I <u>will</u> still excited! (a)Are you knowing Shikoku? Shikoku (b)was the fourth-largest island of Japan. I was so happy when I heard we would visit Shikoku, because I love udon so much. You know what? I ate udon five times during the two-day trip! I (c)have eaten the last one at two p.m. on the second day, when we were to leave in no time. My teacher shouted, "(d)Hurried up, or you are going to be left behind!" I panicked, but it was fun.

②　何がおかしいか	③　正しい英語
（例）前後関係から「まだ興奮している」のは現在の状態として表現するのが自然。	*am* または省略形の *'m*
(a)	
(b)	
(c)	
(d)	

12　Speed Writing／Discussion／Presentation

（1）クラス内で指示された課題について、クラスメートと話し合ってみましょう。

（2）話し合いの内容をもとにして、指定された時間内に指定された語数以上で自分の考えを書いてみましょう。この Unit で学んだ文法事項を意識して文章を作ってください。それ以外は文法事項にこだわり過ぎず、できる限り多くの英文を気楽に書いてみましょう。

（3）自分の考えた文章をクラスメートの前で発表してみましょう。

00 **Grammar：分詞について**

●分詞には、進行や恒常的状態・分類的特徴を表す現在分詞（動詞 ＋ -ing：〜している、
〜する）と受動や完了を表す過去分詞（動詞 ＋ -ed［規則動詞の場合］：〜された、〜さ
れている、〜した）があります。どちらにも名詞の前または後ろから名詞を直接修飾する
限定用法と文中で補語の働きをする叙述用法があります。

☞(1) 限定用法

   (a) a <u>barking</u> dog　　　　　　　　　吠える犬

   (b) the dog <u>barking</u> in the garden　　庭で吠えている犬

   (c) a <u>stolen</u> bag　　　　　　　　　　盗まれたカバン

   (d) the bag <u>stolen</u> by John　　　　　ジョンによって盗まれたカバン

☞(2) 叙述用法

   (e) I heard a dog <u>barking</u> in the garden.　　犬が庭で吠えているのが聞こえた。

     S　V　　O　現在分詞

      （O と現在分詞は主語と述語の関係。　A dog was barking in the garden.）

●知覚動詞（see, hear, smell, feel など）や keep, leave などが、このような形をとります。

01 **Vocabulary（1）：語彙を増やしましょう。**

A. 音声を聴いて、次の表現の発音を確認しましょう。その後、その意味を知らない場合
は辞書を使って調べましょう。次に全ての語句の意味を解答用紙に記入しましょう。 **35**

1. right	2. conversation	3. sure	4. afraid
5. pronunciation	6. importance	7. carefully	8. so that
9. follow-up	10. for example	11. follow up with	12. favorite
13. avoid	14. plan to	15. worry about	16. try -ing
17. clearly	18. English-speaking	19. brave	20. nervous

B. 次の表現は A に入っている単語を定義したものです。それぞれどの単語の定義なのかを考えて、
このテキストに答えとなる単語を書き込んでみましょう。

定義	答え
1. the way in which a particular person makes the sounds of the words of a language	
2. liked more than others of the same kind	
3. having or showing courage	

定義	答え
4.　a spoken exchange of news and ideas between people	
5.　to prevent something bad from happening	

02　Reading／Listening：文章の大まかな意味をつかんでみましょう。

◎英語での会話を途切れさせずに続ける秘訣について、エミさんは、次のような質問をしました。

> I work with some native speakers of English. I want to practice speaking with them so I improve my English. But sometimes, I get nervous, so our conversation ends quickly. How can I talk with these friends for a longer time?

この質問に対する回答をまずは音声で聴いてみましょう。一回目はテキストの文章に注意を払いながら聴いてみましょう。二回目は音声を聴いて１から８のカッコに入る表現を考えながら聴き、書き入れてみましょう。

You are right. It is not always easy to keep a conversation going in English. You might not be（1.　　　）about what to say. Or maybe you are（2.　　　　）that your pronunciation is not good.

Listen and follow up

First, remember the importance of listening. (a)<u>Listen to the other person carefully, so that you can ask a follow-up question.</u> For（3.　　　）, let's say the other person tells you, "I just got back from a trip to Canada."

You can follow up with a question using Who, What, Where, When, Why, or How:

- Where did you（4.　　　）in Canada?
- What was your favorite place there?
- How was the（5.　　　）there?

Avoid simple 'yes' or 'no' questions

(b)<u>If you want to keep a conversation going, it's a good idea to ask questions that cannot be answered with a simple 'yes' or 'no.'</u>

If the other person asks you a 'yes' or 'no' question, try to give a longer answer to help keep the conversation going.

For example, a friend might ask, "Hey, have you

How's everything?

Not too bad.

seen the new Star Wars movie?"

You could just answer, "No, I haven't." Or, you could say more.

You could answer: "No, but I (6.　　　　) to see it soon. How about you?"

Be brave and practice often

Do not (7.　　　　) about your pronunciation. If your pronunciation is a little different, the other person will still understand your message if you try speaking slowly and (8.　　　　).

(c)When you are traveling in an English-speaking country and have some free time, be brave and speak in English with someone who does not look too busy. You may make a new friend.

03 本文中に出てくる「現在分詞」を 3 つ探して、下線を引いてみましょう。

04 Comprehension Questions：

単語の意味をある程度知った上で文章を見ると、理解度が高まることが実感できたのではないでしょうか。では内容の確認をしてみましょう。

次の各文の内容が本文の内容と一致している場合は T を、一致していない場合は F を選び、解答用紙に○をつけましょう。また本文のどの部分を見れば、判断ができるかについても解答用紙に記入しましょう。

(1) It is always easy to continue a conversation in English.
(2) Listening to the other person is not important in conversation.
(3) If you get a yes-no question, it is better to give a longer answer to continue the conversation.
(4) Even if your pronunciation is a bit different, you will still be able to make yourself understood by speaking slowly and clearly.
(5) While traveling in an English-speaking country, you should try to talk with someone in English.

05 Summary

次の文章は本文の内容をまとめたものです。（　　）内に入る表現の最初の文字を書き出してあります。それをヒントに、本文の中から適切な表現を選んで書き入れましょう。

Speaking English can be difficult, and keeping a conversation going is not easy. A few ways to do this are: listen and follow up, (1. a　　　　) simple 'yes' or 'no' questions, and practice often. Listening and following up with WH-questions are good ways to get more information and are better than yes or no questions. Even when someone asks a 'yes' or 'no' question, give longer answers too. Finally, be (2. b　　　　) and challenge yourself to speak, do not worry about pronunciation.

06 Translation（1）

本文中の下線部（a）から（c）を日本語に訳してみましょう。訳は解答用紙に書き入れましょう。

07 Translation（2）

次の文中にはこの Unit でこれまでに見てきた表現が含まれています。気をつけながら日本語に訳してみましょう。知らない表現は辞書で調べて、訳は解答用紙に書き入れましょう。

（1）My cousin is afraid that she may not be able to see her parents again.
（2）He is sure of winning the prize this time.
（3）She did her best to avoid crowded places while shopping.
（4）His words kept her going while she was in prison.
（5）When you give a presentation, speak clearly and slowly with good eye contact.

■ 休憩

●「keep ＋ O ＋ -ing（O を～にしておく）」は、現在分詞の叙述用法です。以下の文では、目的語 "me" を "talking" の状態にしておいたという意味です。
　☞ He kept me talking.（彼は私に話を続けさせた。）
●同様に、本文にある "keep a conversation going" は、"a conversation" を "going" の状態にしておくこと、つまり、continue（続ける）を意味しています。

08 Word Order：

A. 次の ［ ］ 内の表現を日本語に合うように並べ替えてみましょう。分詞の使い方を意識しながら考えてみてください。冒頭は大文字で書き始め、答えは解答用紙に記入しましょう。

（1）英語を話す際は、間違えることを心配しないで。
［ making, worry about, mistakes when, don't, speaking English ］.
（2）スタジアムで野球をしているあの少年は、私の兄です。
［ in the stadium, playing baseball, that boy, my elder brother, is ］.
（3）英国のパブ（居酒屋）で出されるジャガイモの丸焼きは、ジャケット・ポテトと呼ばれる。
［ called, baked potatoes, served in British pubs, are, jacket potatoes ］.

(4) ダンは、注意深く自然を観察することが重要だということに気づいた。
[the importance of, nature carefully, Dan, observing, noticed].
(5) 卒業後は英語圏で働くつもりだ。
[work, in an English-speaking, I, country after graduation, plan to].

B. 並べ替えたものが合っているどうかを、音声を聴いて確かめてみましょう。間違いがある場合は、自分の答えがなぜ間違いなのかを考えてみましょう。

09 Vocabulary（2）：語彙を増やしましょう。

次の日本語表現の意味に合う英語表現を結びつけてみましょう。選んだ答えの表現を解答欄に書き入れましょう。

1. ギターを弾く	2. 先日	3. スーパー
4. 待つ	5. 結局〜することになる	6. 舞台
7. 万引きする	8. 〜を呼ぶ	9. 長い間

> **語群** call, stage, the other day, for a long time, supermarket, end up -ing, play the guitar, shoplift, wait

Vocabulary（2）の表現を使って、次の日本語を英語にしてみよう。ヒントを参考にしてみましょう。

10 **Composition：作った英文は解答用紙に記入しましょう。**

(1) 舞台でギターを弾いているあの男の人を知っていますか。 *現在分詞を使ってみましょう。

(2) 先日少年がスーパーで万引きしているのを見かけた。 *see ＋ O ＋ 現在分詞を使ってみましょう。

(3) 彼は山中で自分の名前が呼ばれるのを聞いた。 *hear ＋ O ＋ 過去分詞を使ってみましょう。

(4) 彼女は結局私を長い間待たせることになった。
*keep ＋ O ＋ 現在分詞（O を〜にしておく）を使ってみましょう。

11 **Exercise: 形容詞化した現在分詞と過去分詞**

●形容詞化した現在分詞と過去分詞を混同しないで正しく使えるようになりましょう。
主語が何なのかを考えてみると、どちらを使うのが適切なのかがわかるでしょう。
☞現在分詞の場合：感情を引き起こす原因となる物や人が主語となります。
☞過去分詞の場合：感情を抱く人が主語となります。

☞次の各文の （ ） 内の選択肢の中から、適切な方を選んで〇で囲み、文を完成させましょう。

(1) This movie is very （ exciting ／ excited ）.

(2) We were （ disappointing ／ disappointed ） with his decision.

(3) I was （ annoying ／ annoyed ） by some students chatting in the library.

(4) That earthquake was really （ frightening ／ frightened ）.

12 **Speed Writing／Discussion／Presentation**

(1) クラス内で指示された課題について、クラスメートと話し合ってみましょう。

(2) 話し合いの内容をもとにして、指定された時間内に指定された語数以上で自分の考えを書いてみましょう。この Unit で学んだ文法事項を意識して文章を作ってください。それ以外は文法事項にこだわり過ぎず、できる限り多くの英文を気楽に書いてみましょう。

(3) 自分の考えた文章をクラスメートの前で発表してみましょう。

00 **Grammar：比較表現について**

●比較表現とは、形容詞または副詞を用いて、人や物の様子や動作を比べることです。比較
表現には、「原級（同等比較）」「比較級」「最上級」があり、比較級、最上級では主に -er
(est) 型と more (most) 型があります。

☞原級（同等）比較：as 形容詞 / 副詞　as 比較対象

　(1) This train is as fast as that one.　この電車はあの電車と同じくらい速い。

☞比較級：形容詞・副詞 er / more 形容詞・副詞　than 比較対象

　(2) This train is faster than that one.　この電車はあの電車よりも速い。

☞最上級：(the)形容詞・副詞 est / most 形容詞・副詞　in 場所 / of 人数

　(3) This train is the fastest（形容詞：速い）in Japan.　この電車は日本で一番速い。

　(4) He can run fastest（副詞：速く）of the three.　彼はこの三人の中で一番速く走れる。

01 **Vocabulary（1）：語彙を増やしましょう。**

A. 音声を聴いて、次の表現の発音を確認しましょう。その後、その意味を知らない場合
は辞書を使って調べましょう。次に全ての語の意味を解答用紙に記入しましょう。

1. during	2. light	3. nearly	4. not ～ at all
5. save	6. prepare	7. most	8. preference
9. product	10. cereal	11. manufacture	12. process
13. grain	14. pour	15. favorite	16. bagel
17. bake	18. somewhat	19. diverse	20. while

B. 次の表現は A に入っている単語を定義したものです。それぞれどの単語の定義なのかを考え
て、このテキストに答えとなる単語を書き込んでみましょう。

定義	答え
1. something that is not heavy, or not very much and great	
2. something or someone you like more than another thing or person	
3. to cook something	
4. to keep something so that you can enjoy or use it later *so that～ can... ＝ ～が…できるように	
5. very different from each other	

◎ "American breakfast" について、ユリコさんは次のような質問をしました。

I wonder how the usual American breakfasts go. What do Americans **prefer** to eat in the morning?

この質問に対する回答をまずは音声で聴いてみましょう。一回目はテキストの文章に注意を払いながら聴いてみましょう。二回目は音声を聴いて１から８のカッコに入る表現を考えながら聴き、書き入れてみましょう。

The usual breakfast

During the work week, many Americans have a (1.   ) breakfast. In fact, nearly 40 percent will not have anything (2.   ) all. (a) Americans usually save larger breakfasts for the weekend, when they have more time in the morning to cook.

The most popular breakfast food is eggs. Americans prepare eggs in many ways. Most people have a preference for how they are cooked. Some Americans eat their eggs with bacon or sausage, meat (3.   ) that often come from pigs.

Another popular breakfast food is cereal - a product manufactured from processed cereal grains. It is usually eaten with milk (4.   ) over it.

Another (5.   ) is hot coffee. Many people have this with a bagel or a donut. A bagel is a baked good made in the shape of a circle or ring. It is heated until the bread is somewhat (6.   ) on the outside, but soft on the inside. Donuts, like bagels, are ring-shaped. But they are cooked in oil and have a sweet taste.

The United States is culturally (7.   ), and you can find so many (8.   ) of food. (b) So, while eggs and meat are popular, millions of Americans eat other things for breakfast.

Brunch

On weekends, people have more time to cook and eat. Many Americans may enjoy a meal we call "brunch" on a weekend day. (c) That word combines "breakfast" and "lunch" – the term for a mid-day meal. Brunch is usually a larger meal than the weekday breakfast. Americans have coffee, fruit juice and sometimes even alcoholic drinks with brunch.

04 Comprehension Questions：

単語の意味をある程度知った上で文章を見ると、理解度が高まることが実感できたのではないでしょうか。では内容の確認をしてみましょう。

次の各文の内容が本文の内容と一致している場合は T を、一致していない場合は F を選び、解答用紙に〇をつけましょう。また本文のどの部分を見れば、判断ができるかについても解答用紙に記入しましょう。

（1） On weekdays, Americans eat larger breakfasts than weekends.
（2） For breakfast, eggs are as popular as cereal in America.
（3） Many Americans eat bacon more than sausages.
（4） A bagel is made like a donut and heated until it is harder on the outside than inside.
（5） There are various kinds of breakfast in America.

05 Summary

次の文章は本文の内容をまとめたものです。（　）内に入る表現の最初の文字を書き出してあります。それをヒントに、本文の中から適切な表現を選んで書き入れましょう。

There is a（1.　d　　　　）number of preference when it comes to American breakfast. During the week Americans tend to enjoy light meals that include popular choices such as eggs, bacon, sausage, and（2.　c　　　　）. Another favorite is hot coffee. On the weekend Americans may also have a heavier meal called brunch which is "breakfast" and "lunch" combined to make a single word.

06 Translation（1）

本文中の下線部（a）から（c）を日本語に訳してみましょう。訳は解答用紙に書き入れましょう。

07 Translation（2）

次の文中にはこの Unit でこれまでに見てきた表現が含まれています。気をつけながら日本語に訳してみましょう。知らない表現は辞書で調べて、訳は解答用紙に書き入れましょう。

（1）Many Americans eat a lighter breakfast on the weekdays.

（2）Cereal is more popular breakfast food than rice.

（3）A bagel or a donut is the best breakfast when you are busy.

（4）Americans love hamburgers as much as hot dogs.

（5）Eggs and meat are eaten most often for breakfast.

■ 休憩

● y で終わる形容詞は「ier / iest」を、e で終わる単語は「r / st」を語尾につけましょう。–ful や –tive など接尾辞のつく単語やつづりの長い単語は more/most 型になります。
☞ happy - happier - happiest
☞ beautiful - more beautiful - most beautiful
● その他、一部には -er/-est や more/ most 型以外の変化をするものもあります。
☞ good - better - best

08 Word Order：

A. 次の ［　］ 内の表現を日本語に合うように並べ替えてみましょう。比較表現の作り方を意識しながら考えてみてください。冒頭は大文字で書き始め、答えは解答用紙に記入しましょう。

（1）今年は去年よりたくさん雨が降った。

[this year, than, we had, last year, more rain].

（2）この問題はあの問題よりも難しい。

[this question, is, that one, than, more difficult].

（3）あの映画は世界で一番人気がある。

[in the world, popular, that movie, is, the most].

(4) 野菜を食べることは、スナックを食べるよりも健康的だ。
[healthier, eating vegetables, than, is, eating snacks].
(5) お茶碗一杯のご飯はパンケーキと同じくらいのカロリーだ。
[has, as many calories, a bowl of rice, as a pancake].

B. 並べ替えたものが合っているどうかを、音声を聴いて確かめてみましょう。間違いがある場合は、自分の答えがなぜ間違いなのかを考えてみましょう。

09 Vocabulary（2）：語彙を増やしましょう。

次の日本語表現の意味に合う英語表現を結びつけてみましょう。選んだ答えの表現を解答欄に書き入れましょう。

1. 〜なので	2. 習慣、くせ	3. 寝坊
4. より少ない	5. 食欲	6. ワッフル
7. 一番に	8. 提供する（される）	9. 民族的に

語群　waffle, best, appetite, oversleeping, as, habit, ethnically, less, offer（ed）

Vocabulary（2）の表現を使って、次の日本語を英語にしてみよう。ヒントを参考にしてみましょう。

10 Composition：作った英文は解答用紙に記入しましょう。

（1）私は寝坊の癖があるので、朝に調理している時間が少ししかありません。

（2）ティムは兄よりも大食漢だ。

（3）私はすべてのアメリカの朝食の中で、そのホテルで提供されるワッフルが一番好きだ。

（4）アメリカ合衆国は民族的に日本よりも多様である。

11 Exercise：比較表現が使われているクイズを読んで正解だと思うものに〇をつけましょう。

（1）Is Tokyo Skytree three times higher than Tokyo Tower?		［ Yes. ／ No. ］
（2）Which is more popular in the United States, basketball or soccer?		［ basketball ／ soccer ］
（3）Which is the longest river in the world?		［ the Nile ／ the Mississippi ］
（4）Can lions run faster than cheetahs?		［ Yes. ／ No. ］

12 Speed Writing／Discussion／Presentation

（1）クラス内で指示された課題について、クラスメートと話し合ってみましょう。

（2）話し合いの内容をもとにして、指定された時間内に指定された語数以上で自分の考えを書いてみましょう。この Unit で学んだ文法事項を意識して文章を作ってください。それ以外は文法事項にこだわり過ぎず、できる限り多くの英文を気楽に書いてみましょう。

（3）自分の考えた文章をクラスメートの前で発表してみましょう。

UNIT **14** ▶▶ **Trust or Believe?**

00 Grammar：仮定法について

●仮定法 ＝「ありえないこと」「仮にこうだったら…」と、現実ではなく仮の世界の話をしたいときに使います。まずは if 節を用いた基本のパターンを学びましょう。

☞（1）仮定法過去「もし〜なら…なのに」

If I <u>were</u> a bird, I <u>would</u> fly to you.
鳥だったら君のところへ飛んでいくのに。

> If ＋ S′ ＋ 動詞の過去形, S ＋ would 等 ＋ 動詞の原形

→ If 節の過去形、主節の助動詞の would, could など<u>助動詞の過去形</u>で、現実と離れている感じを出します。

☞（2）仮定法過去完了「もし〜だったら…だったのに」

If you <u>had left</u> earlier, you <u>could have caught</u> the bus.
早く出発していればバスに乗れたのに。

> If ＋ S′ ＋ had ＋ 過去分詞, S ＋ would 等 ＋ have ＋ 過去分詞

→仮定法過去を、もう 1 段階過去にするイメージです。

●直説法 ＝「ありえること」→現実にありえる話をするときは仮定法ではないので注意！

☞ If it rains tomorrow, I will stay home.
明日雨なら、家にいます。

01 Vocabulary（1）：語彙を増やしましょう。

A. 音声を聴いて、次の表現の発音を確認しましょう。その後、その意味を知らない場合は辞書を使って調べましょう。次に全ての語の意味を解答用紙に記入しましょう。

1. either	2. persuade	3. whether	4. accept
5. likely	6. depend	7. pick	8. add
9. force	10. example	11. past	12. until
13. might	14. expert	15. subject	16. suggest
17. verify	18. earn	19. response	20. deal

B. 次の表現は A に入っている単語を定義したものです。それぞれどの単語の定義なのかを考えて、このテキストに答えとなる単語を書き込んでみましょう。

定義	答え
1. a person with special knowledge, skill or training in something	

定義	答え
2. an arrangement or an agreement, for example in business or politics	
3. to make somebody do something by giving them good reasons for doing it	
4. to discover whether something is correct or true	
5. to put something with something else to increase the number or amount or to make it more important	

02 Reading／Listening：文章の大まかな意味をつかんでみましょう。

◎ "trust" と "believe" の違いについて、クミコさんは次のような質問をしました。

"Trust me" or "believe me?"
When I try to make my friend understand I am right with what I say, which one of these two phrases, should I use?

この質問に対する回答をまずは音声で聴いてみましょう。一回目はテキストの文章に注意を払いながら聴いてみましょう。二回目は音声を聴いて1から8のカッコに入る表現を考えながら聴き、書き入れてみましょう。

You can use either（1.　　　　）to try to persuade your friend. But whether or not your friend accepts what you say likely（2.　　　　　）on how long you have known each other. Trust usually comes with time.

Let's look at an example.

You tell your friend, *"Believe me, I know how to pick the best-winning（3.　　　　）team."*

Here, you are using "believe me" to add（4.　　　　）to your point.（a)But in order to really convince your friend, you will likely have to show a few examples of how you have been right in the past. Until you prove it, he（5.　　　　） not *trust* that you know what you are talking about.

Here is another example:

Your friend sells bicycles for a living. You know she is an（6.　　　　）on the subject.（b)Her experience means you *trust* her opinion when she takes you to buy a bicycle.

"Reza," she says, *"trust me, this is a really good bike for the price. If I were you, I would buy it."*

She is also using "trust me" to add force to her point. But here, (c)she is suggesting that you do not need to verify, or check, to see if what she says is true. She has already earned your trust. So your（7.　　　　）may be:

"I trust you! If you think this bike is a good（8.　　　　　）, then I am ready to buy it. I want it in red!"

We hope you trust us to answer your questions!

03 本文中から「仮定法」が使われている文を 1 つ見つけ、下線を引いてみましょう。

04 Comprehension Questions：

単語の意味をある程度知った上で文章を見ると、理解度が高まることが実感できたのではないでしょうか。では内容の確認をしてみましょう。

次の各文の内容が本文の内容と一致している場合は T を、一致していない場合は F を選び、解答用紙に〇をつけましょう。また本文のどの部分を見れば、判断ができるかについても解答用紙に記入しましょう。

（1） If you want to persuade your friend, you cannot use "believe."
（2） Your friend will more likely accept what you say if you have known each other for a long time.
（3） Until you show a few examples of how you have been right in the past, your friend might not *trust* that you know what you are talking about.
（4） If your friend is an expert on bikes and says "If I were you, I would buy it," your response may be "I believe you," not "I trust you."
（5） You might feel more convinced if your friend says "trust me" than "believe me."

05 Summary

次の文章は本文の内容をまとめたものです。（　）内に入る表現の最初の文字を書き出してあります。それをヒントに、本文の中から適切な表現を選んで書き入れましょう。

You can use either "believe me" or "trust me" to try to persuade a friend, but there are other things you should think about. One thing that this depends on is how long you have known each other. "Believe me" tends to add（1.　f　　　　）to a point and might need some examples of being right in the past. If your friend is an（2.　e　　　　）and they say "trust me" about something, it is likely good to trust them.

06 Translation（1）

本文中の下線部（a）から（c）を日本語に訳してみましょう。訳は解答用紙に書き入れましょう。

07 Translation（2）

次の文中にはこの Unit でこれまでに見てきた表現が含まれています。気をつけながら日本語に訳してみましょう。知らない表現は辞書で調べて、訳は解答用紙に書き入れましょう。

（1）If I were a swallow, I would travel to the southern islands right away.
（2）If you had arrived here five minutes earlier, you could have seen the beautiful rainbow.
（3）If there was one thing I could change about our school, it would be the ridiculous school regulations.
（4）If my friend had not persuaded me to come back, I might have made a terrible mistake.
（5）If she were an angel, what message would I ask her to send to God in heaven?

■ 休憩

●仮定法には、if を使わない表現も色々あります。例を見てみましょう。
☞ Had I money, I would buy it.
もしお金があれば、それを買うのに。
☞ I wish I could speak Chinese.
中国語を話せたらなあ！
☞ Without her help, I couldn't have done the work.
彼女の助けなしに、その仕事はできなかった。
☞ He looks pale as if he saw a ghost.
あたかも幽霊を見たかのように彼は青ざめている。

08 Word Order：

A. 次の［ ］内の表現を日本語に合うように並べ替えてみましょう。（3）～（5）は if 節を使わない仮定法です。冒頭は大文字で書き始め、答えは解答用紙に記入しましょう。

（1）もし太陽が西から昇ったとしても、彼女の鉄の意思は揺るがないだろう。
［ rose, in, the west, the sun, if ］, ［ her iron, would never, will, shaken, be ］.
（2）もしクレオパトラの鼻がもう少し低かったら、世界の歴史は違っていたかもしれない。
［ a little lower, Cleopatra's nose, been, if, had ］, ［ of the world, been different, might, the history, have ］.

（3）あたかも魔法にかかったかのように、彼は一晩で名曲を書き上げた。

［ he had, he wrote, been under a spell, a musical masterpiece in one night, as if ］.

（4）タイムマシーンを持っていたら、恐竜を見るために2億年前に旅するのになあ。

［ a Time Machine, I, had ］, ［ million years ago, dinosaurs, in order to see, travel back two hundred, I would ］.

（5）もし彼女がそのコーチに出会っていなければ、グランドスラムを達成できなかったでしょう。

［ not, the coach, had, she, met ］, ［ could never, she, completed, a grand slam, have ］.

B. 並べ替えたものが合っているどうかを、音声を聴いて確かめてみましょう。間違いがある場合は、自分の答えがなぜ間違いなのかを考えてみましょう。

09 Vocabulary（2）：語彙を増やしましょう。

次の日本語表現の意味に合う英語表現を結びつけてみましょう。選んだ答えの表現を解答欄に書き入れましょう。

1. 昼間	2. 天の川	3. 実現する
4. 少しの	5. 透明な	6. 北斗七星
7. あのとき	8. 勇気	9. 最後の

語群 at that time, a little bit of, the Big Dipper, daytime, last, invisible, courage, the Milky Way, come true

Vocabulary（2）の表現を使って、次の日本語を英語にしてみよう。ヒントを参考にしてみましょう。

10 Composition：作った英文は解答用紙に記入しましょう。

(1) 透明人間だったらいいのになあ。*wish を使ってみましょう。

(2) 太陽がなければ、私たちは昼間に北斗七星や天の川が見えるのに。

(3) あのとき君に少しの勇気があったなら、私たちの夢は実現したかもしれないんだ。

(4) 今日が人生最後の日だったら、君は何を食べる？

11 Exercise：以下は、ウィリアム・バトラー・イェイツ（William Butler Yeats）という詩人による "He wishes for the cloths of heaven" という作品の抜粋です。貧しくても愛する人に素敵なものを捧げたいという気持ちが、仮定法を使って表現されています。和訳を参考に、語群から適切な語を選び、空欄に入れましょう。冒頭は大文字にしましょう。

(1.   )(2.   ) the heavens' embroidered cloths,

Enwrought with golden and silver light,

(3.   )(4.   )(5.   ) the cloths under your feet:

But I, being (6.   ), have only my dreams;

I have spread my dreams under your feet;

Tread (7.   ) because you tread (8.   ) my dreams.

　語群：［ would, had, I, I, spread, on, softly, poor ］

もし僕に、金や銀の光を織り込んだ、天を刺繍した布があったなら、君の足元にその布を広げよう。でも僕は貧しくて、持っているのは夢ばかり。僕の夢を君の足元に広げたよ。
そっと歩いてください、だって君は僕の夢の上にいるのだから。

*embroidered 刺繍された、*enwrought 織り込んだ、*tread 歩く、行く

12 Speed Writing／Discussion／Presentation

(1) クラス内で指示された課題について、クラスメートと話し合ってみましょう。

(2) 話し合いの内容をもとにして、指定された時間内に指定された語数以上で自分の考えを書いてみましょう。この Unit で学んだ文法事項を意識して文章を作ってください。それ以外は文法事項にこだわり過ぎず、できる限り多くの英文を気楽に書いてみましょう。

(3) 自分の考えた文章をクラスメートの前で発表してみましょう。

00 Grammar：関係詞（関係代名詞・関係副詞）について

●関係詞は、名詞を説明する二つの文をつなげる役割をします。主に who, whose, whom, that などの関係代名詞と when, why, where, how などの関係副詞に分かれます。

●どの関係代名詞を使うかは、（1）説明される名詞（先行詞）が人か人以外か（2）関係詞の役割（主格・目的格・所有格）で決まります。

☞ I have a sister. と She speaks Spanish. という文を一つにする場合

人を表す主格の関係代名詞 who を使い、I have a sister who speaks Spanish. となります。

●関係副詞は先行詞が「時」「理由」「場所・状況」または「方法・様子」によってそれぞれ when, why, where, how を使い分けます。

☞ This is the town. と I was born in this town. を一つにする場合

場所を表す関係副詞 where を使って、This is the town where I was born. とできます。

01 Vocabulary（1）：語彙を増やしましょう。

A. 音声を聴いて、次の表現の発音を確認しましょう。その後、その意味を知らない場合は辞書を使って調べましょう。次に全ての語句の意味を解答用紙に記入しましょう。

1. conversation	2. coworker	3. workplace	4. specific
5. guess	6. time off	7. situation	8. weekend
9. suggestion	10. vacation	11. several	12. leave
13. meeting	14. others	15. finally	16. simply
17. understand	18. exit	19. expression	20. common

B. 次の表現は A に入っている単語を定義したものです。それぞれどの単語の定義なのかを考えて、このテキストに答えとなる単語を書き込んでみましょう。

定義	答え
1. a person who works at the place where you work	
2. to go out of a place or situation	
3. relating to a particular individual or situation	
4. an informal talk involving two people or a small group of people	
5. to suppose or think	

◎職場の３つの場面で、同僚と別れる時にそれぞれ何と言えばいいかを、イクミさんが質問しています。

1. When leaving a coworker in the morning
2. When leaving a coworker in the middle of the day
3. When leaving a coworker as you exit the workplace for the day

この質問に対する回答をまずは音声で聴いてみましょう。一回目はテキストの文章に注意を払いながら聴いてみましょう。二回目は音声を聴いて１から８のカッコに入る表現を考えながら聴き、書き入れてみましょう。

I lived in Japan, so I understand why you have this question. In your language, there are （1.　　　　　）expressions people always use for such times. (a)In English, though, there are several different things we can say when leaving someone. You（2.　　　）at some of them in your email:

You said, "Maybe I should have said, 'Have a good one,' 'Nice talking to you,' or 'Enjoy your time off.'"

Situation 1

Let's look at situation 1: You are（3.　　　）a coworker, but you will see him or her at lunch time. In a school, someone may say to a teacher, "Have a good class," or "See you after class." If you are not speaking to a teacher, you can say, "See you at lunch," "See you a little later," or（4.　　　　）, "Later."

See you later
OK!

Situation 2

In situation 2, you had lunch with a coworker and are leaving for the afternoon. Now you can say, "Have a good afternoon." You can also say "Have a good one." That is the same as telling someone to have a good day, afternoon or evening.

Situation 3

Let's look at situation 3, where you are leaving for the evening or weekend. On Fridays, you can always say, "Have a good weekend." On any other（5.　　　　）, you can say, "Good night" or "See you tomorrow."

Let me excuse myself.
Sure

There is one more time when you may want to say something. When you leave a（6.　　　）, you can say to others, "See you later."

Your suggestion, "Nice talking to you" is more（7.　　　　）

see you tomorrow!
Bye !

when you don't talk to someone every day. (b)If you called a friend, for example, whom you have not seen for months, this would be a good way to close the conversation.

"Enjoy your time off" is something we often say to people who are taking days off from work for（8.　　　　　）. This would not be said every day.

(c)And, finally, in any work situation, you can also just say, "Bye!"

03 本文中の Situation 3 から最後までの間で、関係詞（関係代名詞と関係副詞）を 4 つ探して、下線を引きましょう。

04 Comprehension Questions：

> 単語の意味をある程度知った上で文章を見ると、理解度が高まることが実感できたのではないでしょうか。では内容の確認をしてみましょう。

次の各文の内容が本文の内容と一致している場合は T を、一致していない場合は F を選び、解答用紙に○をつけましょう。また本文のどの部分を見れば、判断ができるかについても解答用紙に記入しましょう。

（1）　In Japanese, there are several different things we can say when leaving someone.
（2）　"Have a good one" is the same as telling someone to have a good day, afternoon or evening.
（3）　On Mondays, you can always say, "Have a good weekend."
（4）　"Nice talking to you" is more common when you don't talk to someone every day.
（5）　You can say "Enjoy your time off" every day.

05 Summary

次の文章は本文の内容をまとめたものです。（　）内に入る表現の最初の文字を書き出してあります。それをヒントに、本文の中から適切な表現を選んで書き入れましょう。

There are a several ways to tell a coworker you will "see them later." Each depend on the situation. Here are three situations. The first, if you are leaving and will see them at lunch you can say, "see you at lunch" or "see you later." The second, if you are leaving for the afternoon you can say, "have a good one" or "have a good afternoon."（F　　　　　）, if someone is leaving for the weekend you can say "have a good weekend" or if it is a weekday, "have a good night" or "see you tomorrow." When you doubt you can always just say "bye."

06 Translation (1)

本文中の下線部（a）から（c）を日本語に訳してみましょう。訳は解答用紙に書き入れましょう。

07 Translation (2)

次の文中にはこの Unit でこれまでに見てきた表現が含まれています。気をつけながら日本語に訳してみましょう。知らない表現は辞書で調べて、訳は解答用紙に書き入れましょう。

（1）We learned several ways to close conversation in English.
（2）He had lunch with a coworker and is now leaving for a meeting.
（3）I called my teacher whom I have not seen for months.
（4）Jane took 2 weeks off from work for vacation.
（5）I can understand why you are angry with him.

■ 休憩 ....

●次の文のように、目的格で使われるとき関係代名詞は省略することができます。
☞ This is the book (that) I read yesterday.
これは私が昨日読んだ本です。
●また先行詞の the thing(s) と関係代名詞の that を一つにして what で表すことができます。
☞ These are the things that I need.
これらが私の必要なものです
= These are what I need.

08 Word Order：

A. 次の［　］内の表現を日本語に合うように並べ替えてみましょう。関係詞をどこに置けばいいか意識しながら考えてみてください。冒頭は大文字で書き始め、答えは解答用紙に記入しましょう。

（1）その企画に賛成した人はほとんどいなかった。
［ few people, the project, who supported, there were ］.
（2）私には、お母さんが有名な作家の友達がいる。
［ whose mother, is a famous writer, a friend, I have ］.

（3）謝るべき時がある。

［a time, apologize, you should, when, there is］.

（4）私はなぜ彼がパーティーに来なかったのか知らない。

［I don't know, to the party, he didn't come, why］.

（5）ここが、私が育った町です。

［I grew up, the town, this is, where］.

B. 並べ替えたものが合っているどうかを、音声を聴いて確かめてみましょう。間違いがある場合は、自分の答えがなぜ間違いなのかを考えてみましょう。

09 Vocabulary（2）：語彙を増やしましょう。

次の日本語表現の意味に合う英語表現を結びつけてみましょう。選んだ答えの表現を解答欄に書き入れましょう。

1. まさに〜	2. 誰も知らない	3. 興奮する
4. 奇跡	5. 図書館	6. 人
7. くじに当たる	8. 〜が起こる	9. たくさんのこと

> 語群　get excited, person, miracle, win the lottery, library, exactly, happen, many things, nobody knows

> Vocabulary（2）の表現を使って、次の日本語英語にしてみよう。ヒントを参考にしてみましょう。

10 Composition：作った英文は解答用紙に記入しましょう。

（1）図書館の本は私が知らないことをたくさん教えてくれた。
　　*教えてくれた taught me 〜を使ってみましょう。

(2) 誰も奇跡がどのように起こるのか知らない。 *どのようには関係副詞 how を使ってみましょう。

(3) くじに当たった人は非常に興奮した。 *win の過去形 won を使ってみましょう。

(4) これはまさに私が誕生日に欲しかったものです。 *欲しかったものは what I wanted を使ってみましょう。

11 Exercise：関係詞の前のコンマについて考えてみましょう。

☞次の（a）（b）と（c）（d）は、関係詞の前にあるコンマ以外は全く同じ文です。しかし、文の意味には違いがあります。関係詞の前にコンマがある時は、まずコンマまでを最初に訳し、関係詞の後ろは補足の説明として訳すというルールがあるためです。コンマの有無に気をつけて（a）から（d）までを訳し、（1）と（2）の問題に答えましょう。

（a）の訳：
（b）の訳：
（c）の訳：
（d）の訳：

（1）大阪の 2 人以外にも兄弟がいる可能性があるのはどちらの文でしょう。

    （a）She has two brothers who live in Osaka.

    （b）She has two brothers, who live in Osaka.

（2）負傷者がたくさんでたのはどちらの文でしょう。

    （c）There were few people who didn't get injured in the accident.

    （d）There were few people, who didn't get injured in the accident.

        *few ほとんど～ない、 *get injured 怪我をする

12 Speed Writing／Discussion／Presentation

（1）クラス内で指示された課題について、クラスメートと話し合ってみましょう。

（2）話し合いの内容をもとにして、指定された時間内に指定された語数以上で自分の考えを書いてみましょう。この Unit で学んだ文法事項を意識して文章を作ってください。それ以外は文法事項にこだわり過ぎず、できる限り多くの英文を気楽に書いてみましょう。

（3）自分の考えた文章をクラスメートの前で発表してみましょう。

解答用紙

Unit#：＿＿＿＿＿＿　Date：＿＿＿＿＿＿　Student ID#：＿＿＿＿＿＿　Name：＿＿＿＿＿＿

> 英語の語彙・表現を一つでも多く覚えるように頑張りましょう。知っている語彙・表現が増えれば、英語をより身近に感じられるようになります。
> また、しっかりと考えながら課題に取り組み、答え合わせの際には、自分がわからなかったところをきちんとチェックして復習しましょう。

01　Vocabulary（1）A：破線の上に英語表現を書き入れてから、意味を記入しましょう。

1.	2.	3.	4.	5.
6.	7.	8.	9.	10.
11.	12.	13.	14.	15.
16.	17.	18.	19.	20.

04　Comprehension questions：T か F、また本文中のどのあたりから判断できるかについても書き入れてみましょう。

(1) T・F	判断できる箇所：
(2) T・F	判断できる箇所：
(3) T・F	判断できる箇所：
(4) T・F	判断できる箇所：
(5) T・F	判断できる箇所：

06 Translation（1）：日本語訳を記入しましょう。

(a)
(b
(c)

07 Translation（2）：日本語訳を記入しましょう。

(1)
(2)
(3)
(4)
(5)

08 Word Order：並べ替えた英文を記入しましょう。

(1)
(2)
(3)
(4)
(5)

10 Composition：作った英文を記入しましょう。

(1)
(2)
(3)
(4)
(5)

	各 UNIT で用いる Reading 教材タイトル	URL
Unit 1	The Many Kinds of Roads	https://learningenglish.voanews.com/a/the-many-kinds-of-roads-/5818246.html
Unit 2	Ways to Use the Word "Strong"	https://learningenglish.voanews.com/a/ways-to-use-the-word-strong-/5748467.html
Unit 3	How to Count Syllables	https://learningenglish.voanews.com/a/how-to-count-syllables/4739014.html
Unit 4	Is 'Heads Up' Too Informal?	https://learningenglish.voanews.com/a/is-heads-up-too-informal-/5568793.html
Unit 5	When Was Last Tuesday?	https://learningenglish.voanews.com/a/when-was-last-tuesday-/5428379.html
Unit 6	Asking Someone About Their Job	https://learningenglish.voanews.com/a/ask-a-teacher-asking-someone-about-their-job/4598657.html
Unit 7	Long Johns, Gremlins and Big Wheels	https://learningenglish.voanews.com/a/world-war-ii-terms-long-johns-gremlins-and-big-wheels/5551343.html
Unit 8	How Do I Improve My English?	https://learningenglish.voanews.com/a/how-do-i-improve-my-english-/5225657.html
Unit 9	Silent Letters	https://learningenglish.voanews.com/a/silent-letters/5630471.html
Unit 10	Anything and Nothing	https://learningenglish.voanews.com/a/anything-and-nothing/5676353.html
Unit 11	All About 'Develop'	https://learningenglish.voanews.com/a/all-about-develop-/4968971.html
Unit 12	How Do I Continue a Conversation in English?	https://learningenglish.voanews.com/a/how-do-i-continue-a-conversation-in-english/5240355.html
Unit 13	American Breakfast	https://learningenglish.voanews.com/a/american-breakfast/5612538.html
Unit 14	Trust or Believe?	https://learningenglish.voanews.com/a/trust-or-believe-/5174132.html
Unit 15	How Do You Say Goodbye to a Coworker?	https://learningenglish.voanews.com/a/how-do-you-say-goodbye-to-a-coworker-/4908017.html

テキストの音声は、弊社 HP　https://www.eihosha.co.jp/
の「テキスト音声ダウンロード」のバナーからダウンロードできます。

Restart English!
―Through Learning Grammar and Culture―
リスタート・イングリッシュ

2021 年 12 月 1 日　初　版

著　者 ⓒ 安　　田　　優　美
　　　　松　本　恵　美
　　　　船　本　弘　史
　　　　轟　　里　　香
　　　　デ ニ ス・ハ ー モ ン
　　　　長　岡　亜　生
　　　　朴　　育　　美
　　　　奥　村　玲　香
　　　　須　田　久　美　子
　　　　チ　ア　ノ　典　子
　　　　近　藤　千　代
　　　　友　田　奈　津　子
　　　　吉　田　明　代
　　　　杉　原　由　里　子

発 行 者　佐　々　木　　元

発 行 所　株式
　　　　　会社　英　宝　社
〒 101-0032 東京都千代田区岩本町 2-7-7
電話 03-5833-5870　FAX03-5833-5872
https://www.eihosha.co.jp/

ISBN 978-4-269-66063-2 C3582
組版・印刷・製本／日本ハイコム株式会社